More Acclaim for
# Screw Being Shy

"Screw Being Shy is the book I wish I had growing up with social anxiety. This up-lifting, honest and practical book will help you overcome the fears that are holding you back from living the life you are meant to live. Throughout the pages of Screw Being Shy, Mark serves as both a role model and a guide with curating research and voices that prove that anyone can be more authentic, outgoing and confident."
— **Dan Schawbel, author of** *Back to Human, Promote Yourself* **and** *Me 2.0*

"Screw Being Shy will stop you from being your own worst enemy when it comes to relationships and help to clear your connection to the most important people in your life."
— **David Meltzer Co-founder of Sports 1 Marketing,**
**best-selling author, and top business coach**

"Screw Being Shy is a MUST for anyone in the world who faces moments of shy-ness and/or social anxiety looking for a simple yet highly researched and practical solution."
— **Hal Elrod, international keynote speaker and best-selling author**
**of** *The Miracle Morning* **and** *The Miracle Equation*

"Screw Being Shy is a must needed guide for the young to the old for those facing social anxiety and not being sure of themselves in social situations."
— **Chip Conley, New York Times bestselling author**
**and Strategic Advisor of Airbnb**

"The true essence of most great entrepreneurs comes from being grounded in their personal solitude. Mark's book not only shows entrepreneurs how to harness their inner strength and creativity but also serves as a blueprint to work through the highs and lows of personal struggle and professional ambition. Screw Being Shy is a must-read for entrepreneurs and every one of his or her closest advisors."
— **Sharran Srivatsaa, CEO of Kingstone Lane and Creator of 5amClub.net**

"SCREW BEING SHY provides real world, no nonsense advice for anyone dealing with social anxiety. Mark Metry gives the exact playbook he used to go from being unable to speak to strangers in public to becoming a TEDx Speaker and host the world renowned Humans 2.0 Podcast. I highly recommend this book to anyone wanting to overcome shyness as well as those seeking a better understanding of how crippling social anxiety can be."
— **Marcus Aurelius Anderson, High Performance Coach and**
**author of** *The Gift of Adversity*

"Screw Being Shy offers an incredibly helpful conceptualization of the widespread and universal experience of social anxiety. Grounding social anxiety in past psychological trauma and the body's natural fight/flight response to such perceived threat, Mark normalizes this difficult phenomenon for all those who suffer. With this awareness and understanding comes the ability to heal. Mark offers practical tips to help make daily changes to resolve what for many has been a lifetime sentence of social anxiety."

— **Dr. Nicole LePera, Holistic Psychologist (@the.holistic.psychologist)**

"After years of being shy as a kid, I wish the younger version of me had access to Mark's book to guide me alongside the networking and social skills I teach today"

— **Jordan Harbinger, Creator of Jordan Harbinger Show**

"As someone who's helped thousands of leaders become more self-aware and successful, I find Mark's wonderful book to be an essential guide for anyone struggling with shyness and social anxiety, not just at work but in life."

— **Dr. Tasha Eurich, organizational psychologist and New York Times bestselling author of *Insight and Bankable Leadership***

"Screw Being Shy is a raw, revealing, and remarkable guide to building quality relationships, improving your sense of well-being, and making your impact on the world."

—**Nir Eyal, bestselling author of *Indistractable***

# Screw Being Shy: Learn How to Manage Social Anxiety and Be Yourself in Front of Anyone

Mark Metry

Copyright © 2020 Mark Metry

All rights reserved. No portion of this book may be reproduced or transmitted in any form or by any means, electronic or mechanical, including photocopying, recording, or any information storage and retrieval system, without written permission from the publisher.

Published by Mark Metry

ISBN-13: 9798616393241

Printed in the United States of America

# Contents

| | |
|---|---|
| Introduction | 7 |
| **1. Social Anxiety is Not the Problem** | **13** |
| Degrees of Social Anxiety | 13 |
| **2. State of Human Existence** | **21** |
| Neuroscience Behind Our Existence | 25 |
| Truth Is the Chiropractor of the Mind | 29 |
| **3. Life's Greatest Invention** | **33** |
| Death's Greatest Takeaway | 37 |
| **4. Biochemistry Your Biggest Starting Leverage Point** | **41** |
| First My Gut Broke, Then My Brain Broke | 42 |
| A Strong Mind Is Built in the Kitchen | 45 |
| Massive Nutrition Shake | 48 |
| 10 Key Minerals to Reduce Social Anxiety | 49 |
| Rest and Intelligent Exponential Technology | 55 |
| Sleep Like a Baby | 57 |
| 13 Keys to Sleeping like a Baby | 58 |
| Substances of Our Society (Drugs) | 59 |
| Anxiety Says Move | 64 |
| Body <—> Mind Feedback Loop | 66 |
| **5. Learning How to Be Human** | **69** |
| Layers of Social Anxiety | 70 |
| Words are Sort of Meaningless | 71 |
| Pretend You're an Extrovert Sometimes | 73 |
| The Ultimate Learning Highway (FLOW) | 74 |
| Changing the Way you Think About Yourself | 80 |
| The Subtle Art of Not Thinking | 82 |

| | |
|---|---|
| **6. Expose Yourself** | **85** |
| Exposure Therapy | 86 |
| Shyness Alternative Mask and False Confidence | 88 |
| Shame: The Ticking Time Bomb | 90 |
| Meditation Will Crack You Open | 92 |
| **7. Being a Shy Entrepreneur / At Work** | **97** |
| Managing Social Anxiety at Work | 97 |
| Show Yourself to Social Media If You Want | 102 |
| Harnessing Shyness as a Superpower | 104 |
| **8. The World Needs You** | **109** |
| Afterword | 111 |
| References | 113 |

# Introduction

"I don't know what happened, but I think my social anxiety is gone. I just talked to the waitress." – Me, to my sister at a restaurant in 2016.

This was one of the first times in my life, at age 19, when I was in a social situation and was able to say what I wanted, when I wanted, and to whom I wanted without a cage around my brain and mouth like an impending panic attack was about to unfold. Yes, you heard me correctly. I said the first time I've talked to a stranger at the age of 19 without wanting to die. Prior to that moment, whenever I had to go to a store or a restaurant and speak on my own, my brain would go down a spiral of socially anxious thoughts that would try to convince me to not open my mouth. Almost like my brain and existence were rivals, always wanting to suppress me, not value me, tell me I'm worthless to the world and nobody wants to hear me talk. Funny enough, today I host one of the world's biggest podcasts, get paid to speak on stage in front of thousands about my life story, and provide potential solutions that over 30 million people have benefited from.

By reading this book, I want to take you through my journey from being a kid who didn't open his mouth for the first part of his life, to going on a fear dominating conquest for true freedom in my life, and then seeing success come from the outside world for me just being myself. This book is not so much about my detailed life story. This book is meant to serve as the most practical, straightforward guide to help you shed the skin of being a shy person with some level of social anxiety. As we now know, stories are the ways humans have stored facts, data, and emotions for thousands of years, and I plan to do the same in this book. Despite the tidbits of my story, this book is supported with scientific references that back up what I'm saying, alongside my practical knowledge. My story will be sprinkled throughout this book but will be primarily mentioned in the audiobook version, in between chapters, where my friend will be interviewing me.

I'm not here to waste your time. The worst-case scenario in writing this book is you reading it like you're reading a fictional novel. If you do not stop every once in a while and act on the material I'm talking about, I will consider this project a failure. My goal with this book is to hear from one person who struggles with social anxiety or speaking up or being themselves in front of others and redefines themselves and become successful; however, they define and perceive it in their own lives. I am writing this book because a guide like this doesn't exist. Many previous works from authors before me, including psychologists and human behavioral experts, have written books on similar topics, but I've read them. They don't include the material I had to learn directly from my life experience through experimentation, embarrassment, and falling down on my face again and again and again. As a 22 year old, I'll be honest. I'm a bit wary about writing a book on such a complex topic. However, I've gotten out of my own way and the world needs this book because I see so many people like me suffering from social anxiety, which leads to social isolation, which leads to many other issues, including suicide, where I nearly trod.

We all encounter many problems and struggles throughout our lives. However, I believe social anxiety is one of the worst symptoms of a problem you could face in your life. Why? Maybe I am a bit biased because I lived in a social anxiety cage trapped inside my mind for most of my life. The key to life is how you communicate to yourself and to the rest of the world. When you are afraid to talk to others or to express your true self in social environments, it sets you up for a miserable lifetime of being unable to connect with others. Other problems people face aside from social anxiety are relatively manageable because you can talk to others and ask for help. When you are "shy" or can't talk to people, you try to hide everything about your life from everyone, which leads to a life of quiet desperation, hopelessness, and poor mental health. This is a pervasive problem in our society because it's so detrimental. Most people in the world today are mislabeling people who really struggle with social anxiety and shyness as "being an introvert." If you are an introvert, that's awesome; I'm an introvert too. There's nothing wrong with focusing more time on yourself, but being nervous when you have to speak around others is social anxiety. Unfortunately, we suffer the most because of this mislabeling, but it doesn't have to be this way. There is nothing we can't do together in educating people about social anxiety, and in completing this mission, we can actually change the world and help the state of each person's consciousness around the globe.

Why is this important? Because if you're like me, not talking to the world for 18 years will lead you to having depression, social isolation (which is worse than smoking), severe anxiety in all forms, and even being suicidal at times. In this book, I will break down key fundamentals and coping skills I had to learn to completely change the core of my identity, to recognize who I really am and not who the world tried to label me as. I will lay out the essential steps and tools I utilized both physically and mentally to conceptually understand anxiety and move me forward past living in my own head.

To paint the picture for you, I was born in 1997 and grew up in Boston, Massachusetts,. I know I just said I'm not here to talk about my story, but getting a bit of context and background about me is important. In 1995, my parents immigrated to the United States and didn't know the English language. They came over with just a couple of hundred bucks in their pocket. I grew up with a simple childhood, enjoying the bare necessities and simplicities of life while never thinking as a kid, "Wow, I'm poor and others have more than me."

I was always the crafty, intuitive kid in the back of the classroom that had a tight circle of friends and was always up to something resourceful. I was for sure an introvert, which is defined as a person **predominantly concerned with their own thoughts and feelings** rather than with external things. Introverts gain energy and recharge through alone time. I wasn't shy, just more in my own head, in a good way. It wasn't until I moved schools from the 2nd to 3rd grade that I slowly began developing social anxiety and became the shy kid in the back of the classroom with no friends. My family moved out of the city and into a smaller town in rural western Massachusetts because my parents got better jobs out there. It was a nicer area than where we had lived before with a much better socioeconomic status. I saw mansions and nice cars for the first time in my life.

I remember walking into my first classroom as the new kid at my new school. As I walked through the room, I saw many smiling kids, an amazing 3rd grade teacher who helped me a lot, and I realized that everyone in that classroom was white. I unconsciously realized throughout the hallways and in the cafeteria, almost every single person at my school was white. There were just a few handfuls of other families in the entire town of 5,000 people who also looked physically different like me. I don't want to exaggerate this part of my story because that doesn't do any justice. There were people who showed extraordinary kindness, and there were others who made it clear that I didn't belong. In any social environment, there will be kind people and people who just don't realize the animosity they present through their behavior.

Though I was always an introvert with a tight circle of friends, when I joined my new school, my introversion transformed into extreme shyness. Over the years, I developed severe social anxiety, to the point where I began getting anxious even when I wasn't with people. And when you begin developing anxiety on top of your previously existing condition, it creates a psychological feedback loop that can keep you stuck in your own mind. You could be surrounded by the most loving people in your life but always view yourself as a loner and a loser. And because you believe that about yourself, you will act accordingly.

The kind of social anxiety I'm talking about is whenever I would walk into a room, my brain would tell me "look down", "you don't look like anybody here", "you're never gonna fit in", "find a safe spot in the back of the classroom and don't talk to anybody." Eventually, this got to a point where I had just a small number of "friends", who I became friends with because they were also considered outsiders and not part of any clique. Reality is, they weren't even my friends or people I had a sense of connection with.. I was creating the illusion I had friends, when in reality, I was so lonely. My social anxiety took its toll: I was a terrible student, I couldn't focus in class, I couldn't study, but I couldn't stand to be isolated. Social settings like at lunch in the cafeteria or time at the playground I would spend by myself either sitting down in a corner or walking around.

At the same time, I began to develop many chronic health conditions that many kids today in America face largely classified under autoimmune issues. I began to develop asthma, issues with my stomach, insomnia, random skin rashes, and never being able to focus on anything in my mind or in the outside world. In turn, I was routinely going to the doctor and was prescribed various medications. I was told this is something simple, out of your control, and you should accept it. As I began to take varying medications, my energy got completely zapped to the point where, combined with my social anxiety, it created the ultimate prison inside of my own mind where even if I wanted to talk to people, my brain didn't let me. My mind had a lot of energy, but my body had no energy or capacity to do or express what my brain wanted.

As I was growing up, the shock of 9/11 really began to intrude into the culture of America and the fear of middle eastern immigrants. This is when I began to get bullied. A few times there were physical altercations on the playground where I was shoved to the ground and held down. White kids punched me and insulted me. I remember people would routinely call me a terrorist, that I was related to Osama Bin Laden, and me and my whole family were going to blow up the entire school.

Combined with my social anxiety and health issues, the bullying continued to drive me further down the rabbit hole of being in my own bubble with nobody to talk to and shame bubbling up. I have never done anything violent, never punched anyone, but I began to take on the shame of those bad things not because of what I did, but because of what I looked like. Knowing I couldn't change them or me resulted in general anxiety, where now I would try to hide from everybody, even my friends and family, what I was really going through because fear slowly began to dominate my life.

I have this particular memory of leaving the classroom to go to the restroom. I came back and saw written on my binder "we're gonna kill you sand n*gger. Go hang out with Osama Bin Laden." I went to the principal and they launched an investigation, found out who did it, and reprimanded them. But that didn't erase my psychological trauma. There were many little events leading up to this moment that kept on giving my brain evidence that I was a loser and destined to become a nobody in society, even though deep down I knew I was a kind-hearted person.

My anxiety got so bad I began to develop issues with wetting the bed. I wet the bed not just when I was a kid but until I was 18, when I slowly began to transform myself. If you ever see someone get into a traumatic event or a car accident, they wet themselves. I would believe my anxiety so much that my brain would go into a fight or flight response and trigger. But, on the days I didn't wet the bed, I literally couldn't sleep. I would stay up for a full 8 hours and just go to school the next day like a zombie. This happened every day of my life from ages 9 to 18. I was waging a mental war that would go on inside of my mind, and nobody around me had any idea except for maybe those who were also going through the same thing. We were in the same position, but we couldn't help each other.

Being shy is to avoid doing or becoming involved in (something) due to nervousness or a lack of confidence. If you have NEVER been socially anxious, you should stop reading now, unless you have a loved one who experiences this, and you wish to help them on their journey. Please send this book to anybody young or old who experiences difficulty in speaking their mind. And if that's you right now reading this book, I just want to say I have been there. I have been trapped in what I would describe as a damn hell hole inside of my own mind for over a decade with the feeling that nobody understands you. Trust me: it IS possible to change. It's just going to require you to really want this like you've never wanted something before.

Nobody in my life growing up understood what I was facing, and probably because I couldn't tell them because **I didn't even know I had social anxiety** and lacked the language to articulate what I was feeling. As you continue reading this book, I will go through the layers and thought realizations I had that enabled me to ultimately break out of this prison I had created. Growing up, I thought this was going to be my life forever. When you get trapped into a repetitive bubble every single day, like going to school if you are a student or working a repetitive mundane job, your brain can make you believe that change is impossible, and you are going to be stuck this way forever. This only makes your overall anxiety worsen, which then leads to living a life of quiet desperation.

**The human mind is the worst prison because you don't know where the jail cell starts and ends.**

My entire goal with this book is to get you to take that first step, the first domino within a multitude of elements and forces going on in our lives.

I'm not a scientist. I'm not a psychologist. I'm not a nutritionist. I'm not a behavioral expert. I'm just a person like you, who was able to get on the other side of this hell hole and now I'm trying to help as many people as possible. Because the world does not benefit from you staying quiet, because you help zero people in keeping your mouth shut, and you shouldn't hide your well-intentioned actions.

# 1.

# Social Anxiety is Not the Problem

"Dude, what the hell happened? I just talked to that girl and that guy over there completely fine without hesitation." – Me, drunk at a college party

The first step to solving any problem is to realize you have a problem. I didn't know I had social anxiety up until this moment in college when I was at a party and I got a bit drunk. What I didn't know back then was alcohol shuts down the part of your brain that processes judgment in social settings. This is why some people might wake up the next morning from partying and regret making certain decisions they made. It was this substance induced realization that began to shift my life. Even though drinking is **NEVER** a solution, being without inhibition gave me the awareness that I could do something and step outside of my own bubble for the first time. It gave me the sense that there are different kinds of social anxiety.

## Degrees of Social Anxiety

Before we get started on the first chapter, I want to make a very clear point. There's a big difference between being afraid to express the real you to others and being an introvert. In doing my research for this book, many people told me that being shy is not the same as having social anxiety. I disagree.

There's a difference between being a regular person who may be an introvert but can speak their mind and those without much mental anguish versus somebody who society has deemed shy so many times as the explanation to who they are, they accept the label of "I'm just introverted". Deep down, sometimes these people would love to have a conversation with that interesting person sitting at the table over there or say what they really want to say to their friends and family without their brains dropping a judgmental bomb inside their minds.

Finding out that you have social anxiety is potentially the greatest thing or worst thing to ever happen to you. As a kid, I had no idea I had social anxiety and just thought that there was something wrong with me. The moment when I found out I was socially anxious, I felt a great sense of liberation, almost as if the previous events and moments in my life began to connect and make sense for the first time ever. Instead of using that label as an inhibitor and limit myself even more, I used it as a real liberator. Every time I would feel extremely socially awkward or experience suffocating anxiety, I would just remember that this is happening because I have social anxiety. Understanding this about myself gave me a great sense of peace and clarity, but I never used it as an excuse to remain as I am. Sure, I have nervous system crippling social anxiety, but that's not going stop me from doing what I actually want to be doing with the right kinds of people in my life.

Introvert is defined as a person predominantly concerned with their own thoughts and feelings, rather than external things. I am still an introvert most of the time, while balancing it with moments and spurts of intentional extroversion. If you feel nervousness, trembling, mental panic, confusion, or fear when thinking about speaking to others, you are socially anxious. I am not a fan of labels in general, but it's important to realize social anxiety is not who you are at your core – it's a condition you live with. In fact, there was a study done by psychologists at UCLA in 2007 that shows when you label certain emotions, it biochemically reduces the impact of fear your brain produces. It's like telling yourself next time you walk into a room, and you feel your forehead sweating, chest beating, and thoughts racing, and rather than asking yourself a million questions, you simply recognize your social anxiety is acting up.

A lot of the times being shy is an unconscious excuse to remain invisible. If you think there's something about you that you can't really change, you will live your life not even trying while quietly trying to convince yourself of this false notion. Let me tell you one thing: you, yes YOU, can lie to everyone around you... but you will never be able to lie to yourself. This opens the door of living a life of quiet desperation, not living your own life with peace.

Do you know what the #1 regret is of people on their deathbeds? Bronnie Ware, an Australian nurse working in palliative care, also known as caring for patients in the last 12 weeks of their lives. recorded the top regrets of the dying. She found that the #1 regret is the fact that they lived somebody else's life and didn't have the courage to do anything without doing what others expect from you. Don't die with the unlived version inside of you when right now, whether you are 18, 80, 12, 26, or 56 years old. You have time. Do you really want to be on your deathbed and looking back at every event of your life with regret because you didn't express your soul? Why? Because you were afraid to talk to others because of some long elaborate excuse only you would understand? I'm not being harsh; I'm just being real with you. I wish someone was real with me in my life because I might have been able to create a plan, a vision to help myself become the person I wanted to be earlier on.

In the chapters that follow, I will guide you with the proper conceptual framework and practical application of what you can do to create your own path out of social anxiety and not be a prisoner of your mind or wait on other people to open the door for you.

You most likely decided to purchase or read this book because you want social anxiety to be a thing of the past. You want to talk to people but every time you get a thought to say something, you get another thought that tells you to shut up and locks your mouth shut. You have something to say of importance, but a part of your brain doesn't think so.

Well, the good news is you are already ahead of 99% of people who don't even bother reading or learning because they view themselves in life as a fixed entity. Like a rock that can't move. Have you ever heard of that phrase "a leopard can't change its spots?" Guess what? We're humans, not leopards! Yay! The higher powers in the universe like God, or what you choose to believe have blessed us with the creation of our minds, hearts, and spirits that gives us the ability to think, create, discover, change, and reinvent almost everything about ourselves if we set our mind to it.

I hate to break this to you, but your problem is not actually social anxiety. The problem is not being shy or even lacking confidence. The problem is not that you are in an environment where there might be mean or hostile people. The problem is a much deeper series of complex nodes that help create our existence, and the personal reality you see when you open your eyes. I could've written this book with the simple purpose of defeating your social anxiety and building up your confidence; but that would be superficial and not actually help you get to the root cause of the problem. We need more than band-aid solutions offered by half of the books that exist in the self-help genre.

You accept that the problem is not social anxiety and so you might think to yourself, so the problem is with me? Sort of, but I want to make a clear distinction and say throughout my entire life, because of my social anxiety, I thought there was an issue with me. I believed I was a moral failure born into this earth as a broken soul, which is simply not true. Yet, this untruth makes the degree of anxiety and hopelessness much worse when you believe that you are just destined to be broken.

Almost all of the problems of the human experience involve the way and manner in which we learned what we learned at the beginning of our creation. Believe it or not, if you look at most animals, the moment they are born they can run around and be independent. For us humans, it's a different story. Look at a human baby. It can barely move or do anything on its own other than sleep, poop, and eat. A human baby can't hold its own head up and if left alone for a short time, would cease to exist. That used to be you and me, once upon a time. But now we are adults with those same basic structures of neurons in our brains that got us this far.

When you are born, what happens is our brain and body begins to learn what to do over a period of our first several years of life. Then what happens is our brain is constantly seeking and learning to readily answer the question of "What do I need to do to survive?" Your actions and immediate behaviors in life begin to lay down the foundation of how your brain will wire circuits to create highways of energy that can easily be deployed without thinking about them. Let me give you an example: why does a baby cry? Because it knows it can't help itself, however other people can help a baby. Through thousands of years of survival instinct, babies have learned that if I want something, I need to cry in order to get it. That's how I'm going to survive.

Another example: You are in elementary school. The teacher in your history class assigns a major project about creating a presentation for the class about your favorite historical event. You go back to your house and you remember your grandfather was in the Vietnam war. You make an amazing project about the war and what you learned from it and how personal this event is because of your grandfather. You go to class the next day and present your amazing Vietnam project to your classmates. Your teacher, at the end of the presentation, mentions that you got two of the pivotal years wrong and other information you were "missing" results in a subpar presentation. You feel embarrassed, your cheeks flush red, and you look down to the ground not knowing what to say or how to respond, so you stand in silence. The entire class begins laughing at you for doing so and you walk to the end of your classroom and sit in the back of the class so ashamed and embarrassed. What just happened was you put your heart into something, the world did you wrong, and now your brain is learning about the world and comes up with the conclusion of "Wow. I did my all, but everyone made fun of me. I'm never opening my mouth or trying hard on a project again because if I do the same thing will happen." Most times, our brain draws these conclusions without us even knowing in our conscious minds that we chose to do that.

This, my friends, is what we call psychological trauma.

Psychological trauma can be defined as damage to the mind that occurs as a result of a distressing event. Trauma is often the result of an overwhelming amount of stress that exceeds one's ability to cope, or to integrate the emotions involved with that experience. But it is essentially when something you perceive based on your level of understanding of life so far "goes wrong"; something that you have never faced and don't know how to process. Most people think trauma is only reserved for devastating events like watching someone die, experiencing a violent act, or getting bullied as a young kid. However, based on what we know now, trauma can be much broader and can even extend to things like your parents not being home, getting rejected by a friend, or being insulted or mocked by your classmates and teachers for saying something different than everybody else.

Trauma is such a deep and vast topic that we will not cover it extensively in this book because it is not my area of expertise. For more resources on learning about trauma I recommend the works of the following experts: Mastin Kipp, Dr. Nicole LePera, and Dr. Joe Dispenza.

Frequently when trauma emerges, we seek some sort of temporary relief, comfort, or safety in order to cope with it. Some sort of relief could be a bottle of alcohol, choosing to feel anger, bullying others, or even a repeating story or narrative in your head based on why you think what happened, happened. This is social anxiety. You can lose the ability to live life in the present moment. So, whenever you find yourself in a similar situation, your mind flashes back to that trauma, which can cause you to relive the moments, freeze, pause, get embarrassed, not have clear thoughts in a conversation, etc.

Early in my life, I went through multiple traumatic moments and that led to me thinking, "You know what? I'm sick of this world. I'm not doing this anymore. I'm going to retreat inside of myself and not raise my hand or speak because I could be wrong and that will get me in trouble again." Social anxiety became a MASK I wore so I wouldn't get hurt again. I'm not saying that's you, because I don't know you and everybody in this life is different, but it certainly could be you and not know it.

Most of us would rather keep doing the same thing that we've gotten used to than find and live our truth. On my journey, the hardest part about all of it was getting started. You have to admit that the problem could be psychological in nature. No one is at fault, but you can't change that. It's not your fault you got bullied or you had a good friend of yours betray you. But more often than not, this has happened years, if not decades, ago. Why are you letting something, or someone, impact your life now?

I began getting bullied and faced racial tension during my late elementary and middle school years; that took a toll on my mental health. Nobody bullied me after that in high school, and that's when I was at my worst. Living in the past was no answer for me. Those people, cliques, and bullies could not continue to have power over me. Typing out all of this after the fact sounds so crazy and pointless to me now because I've taken the right steps towards forgiveness, peace, love, health, and prosperity, but it was not common sense doing these things at the time.

If you can begin to understand that you don't need to blame anyone, and maybe you don't know how everything in the world works and how people think, you can find the courage to inch towards the conscious awareness that the truth of what you are doing or how you are acting is probably not the best for the foreseeable future. But, almost nobody does this in our society. We are chained to the jails of comfort and routine. Why have this conversation with yourself when it's about to be 12 o'clock and you can eat lunch? Why should you sit down and do the hard things when at 7 o'clock you're going to go down to the bar with your buddies and have a few drinks?

Unfortunately, most people don't realize they require a massive life changing moment to surrender. Perhaps it's your parents dying in a car accident, or you are looking in the mirror at yourself and seeing you weigh 300 pounds. Some people, even in those moments, choose to cling to comfort because it's easier. It's easier to drink alcohol or smoke something than to actually try to find your unvarnished, real truth. It's hard. Personally, it took me until I was suicidal to actually surrender.

**Try this exercise below to gain more awareness about your shyness:**

**Exercise**: Sit down alone for 15 minutes without distractions. Put your phone in another room and set a timer so you can hear it. Pull out a writing utensil for the prompts below and ask yourself these questions to get you to dig a bit deeper rather than repeating the same things you've told yourself for years.

**What are my vices?** Ex. Video Games, eat junk food, watch porn, get angry at my partner or kids, mindlessly scroll through twitter, binge tv shows, drink alcohol, hang out with the wrong people, etc.

**Remove all your vices for 24 hours.** Answer the following prompts with the same protocol from above and make sure you have removed your vices so you can get in touch with the real, primal essence of your soul.

1. Am I socially anxious?
2. How do I know I am socially anxious?
3. Why do I think I'm shy?
4. Why am I afraid to be the real me?
5. I know I get anxious around others when I feel:

# 2.

# State of Human Existence

Before we explore any further about the fear of what other people will think about us, it's important to understand the very bedrock of human civilization. Throughout my entire life I have always thought that adults, whether it be a family relative, teacher, an authority figure like a police officer, were always right. It wasn't until I grew up and became an adult that I realized that nobody knows what's going on and we're all just doing our best with what we know.

    I wish somebody would have told me this early so that growing up when I heard a teacher scream at me because I got out of line, or I said something in class that wasn't appropriate based on how they perceived it, I wouldn't have taken it so seriously. The truth is that a boss or teacher that yelled at you is the same thing as if you yelled at a child for doing something "wrong" - which really is just your opinion of how the world should work. When I look back at my life, sure I made mistakes; everyone has a past. But, how people react to something you did or didn't do doesn't actually have anything to do with you. Their reactions are about their ideas, their lives, and their emotions.

    Let me explain.

    Are you an original? To some degree you are...the exact ratio of atoms and chemicals that created you is like no other. However, we are all very much the same. We come from the outcry of all of human civilization that has come before us. A thought you have today has more than likely already been thought of by somebody else. Look at human history. I am a practical optimist when it comes to most things in life, but human history is not amazing other than the fact that all events led us to get to this point in society.

History is filled with world wars, genocide, slavery, mass rapes, concentration camps, pillaging, and many horrible things that happened throughout history that happened to bring us here. Human history is also filled with miraculous achievements like relative prosperity around the globe, the advances of agriculture, being able to harness the power of nature, inventing medicine that has saved billions of people's lives, and even flying away from this planet to others in our solar system.

Why am I saying all this? Because the thoughts you think in your mind may not even be yours. Now, obviously they are yours because they come from your brain, a thinking organ that emits 25,000-60,000 thoughts a day. Is it perhaps possible that our thoughts are encoded into our DNA? You come from your mom, who came from her mom, who came from her mom, etc.

In fact, the Emory University School of Medicine conducted a study with mice and found that memories pass between generations. Not just the memories, but also the ramifications. Professor Marcus Pembrey, from University College London, said the findings were "highly relevant to phobias, anxiety, and post-traumatic stress disorders" and provided "compelling evidence" that a form of memory could be passed between generations.

Why do animals just born from the womb already recognize potential predators and know what to do? Researchers and geneticists have suggested that we have hard encoded DNA of the habits and behaviors that were universal across time, like fear, hunting for food, searching for shelter, etc. Perhaps what I find the most fascinating about thoughts is there is no origin point of a thought. We "receive" thoughts, like our brain is a radio with an antenna and a thought is a radio frequency. You turn on the machine and boom! A thought is received. You just thought of something now. And another one. That thought that just went by...were you able to stop it before you thought it? Nope.

BOOM. Thought created and now it's up to you to decide with your consciousness, your point of view of this thought, what to do with it. Depending on how you interact with that feedback loop, it may produce more negative thoughts. Regardless, your brain will always think. You can't shut it off. Thoughts aren't necessarily the big troublemaker we think when it comes to "negative self-talk". The truth is everyone has these thoughts tumbling around.

But, the real point of freedom is how our consciousness can create a profound thought that leads to the emotions and assumptions about life that thought can imply. Just try telling someone to not think negative thoughts.... negative thought... negative thought.... negative thought. Again, that's not the way our psychology has evolved and attempting to only "stop having negative thoughts" will indeed increase the frequency and magnitude of the power of not so great thoughts.

On a side note, if you are reading this and you are thinking to yourself what is this guy talking about? I don't know about any of my thoughts. Heck, I don't even know when I get a thought. I'm not crazy or talking about hearing voices in my head. I'm talking about self-awareness.

You will never be able to shut your brain off entirely. You will never be able to get rid of negative self-talk entirely because that's not the way our brains were designed. Our brains aren't just thinking organs. Over the course of millions of years, our brains have evolved to detect dangers to ensure the survival of the entire organism. Dangers aren't just immediate threats like somebody assaulting you or stealing a possession. Much more complicated dangers, combined with our neocortex (where imagination lies), are able to create vivid predictions of future dangers based on intelligence, which is your memory of past experiences. Our brains are supercomputers and have evolved to perceive the four dimensions of reality and confines of space in combination with innumerable variables a brain must factor to calculate what's going on and what we should be doing right now.

An example threat could be not hitting your sales quota at your job, which means you might not be able to pay all your bills, which then relates to the very safety and well-being of not just yourself but your whole family. Most of these complicated future threats involve our individual interactions in society alongside other people who also have brains. Meaning, your brain doesn't just detect threats in physical reality but has evolved to detect psycho-group identity threats as well, involving the experiences of the past and future with other people in your society. Combining all these factors can create social anxiety.

Here's the truth. Humans were able to survive and become the dominant species on this planet for many reasons, one of them being is that we know how to work together in groups better than any other species. Without exception, if you are not a part of a bigger group and outside in the wilderness, you are more likely to be captured, killed, or even eaten alive. Groups are essential to survival and our minds know that.

The human brain has developed the cognitive hardware to communicate at a very deep level, even passing words and language to the other human. Including other humans that are highly dependent on each other for survival was crucial during ancestral times. Often times, there was a village elder or leader, and if you disagreed with him or her, you would be reprimanded beyond any modern day justice system.

What happens if you speak up to the village elder?

What happens if you do or say something wrong to your village?

What happens if someone doesn't like you because you said something?

You get exiled. You get kicked out of your group. This is cognitively synonymous for you are going to die in nature by yourself. Or even worse, you get kicked out with your family with you and your little children are forced to come with you. Even worse, you are separated from them and the village punishes them separately. Abandoned to die in the wild because you opened your mouth... In fact, researchers from the Department of Psychology at the University of California reported in a study that "emerging evidence has shown that social pain--the painful feelings that follow from social rejection, exclusion, or loss--relies on some of the same neural regions that process physical pain, highlighting a possible physical-social pain overlap".

This is the very simple version of why our evolutionary biology sets the pathway for social anxiety. In today's modern world it's not just the village elder; it could be a teacher, the most popular kid at school, police officers, political leaders, or even your dad. If you have social anxiety and struggle to talk to people, communicating with authority figures is extremely difficult. It's not just that you are shy. Your entire brain and body is triggering an immediate fight or flight emergency response protocol that can't be controlled and you have no choice or freedom in your life. Combine all that with our species past experiences of recorded memories stored in the cell of our bodies, and now your very biological chemistry is working against you.

Like we mentioned above, I'm no expert in genetics. But I believe the same way a giraffe knows what to do right after coming out of the womb, humans are similar in that respect. In fact, a study done by scientists at the Max Planck Institute for Human Cognitive and Brain Sciences in Leipzig, Germany, and the Uppsala University, Sweden confirmed that the human mind naturally fears serpents or snakes. They showed infants pictures of different animals and saw a pattern of drastic stress reactions when shown snakes and spiders. We have stored memory in our cells, that was once probably there for a good reason, for us to survive.

I hope this section was helpful in a bit more on understanding the nature of our existence and the mechanisms at play we may or may not necessarily have control over. However, one thing is clear, and that's the fact that as humans we have the ability to design our thoughts. One tool I used to become conscious of my own thoughts and slowly change them over time is journaling. Every morning after my meditation practice, I will open my iPad and begin writing down my thoughts, ideas, and anything else that pops up in my head. The real power in this is as there are so many thoughts bubbling around in our heads, it's almost impossible to keep track of what we are thinking throughout the day.

Many of those unconscious thoughts are negative and keep us operating and moving at the same level that creates our behavior. What happens if you begin to write those thoughts down on paper? Your brain, a thinking organ, sees what it just created and begins thinking in a different way. You have just created a feedback loop. If you write down what you are grateful for, any ideas you have to improve yourself, any fears or insecurities that are bothering you, eventually your brain will create new thoughts from the previously existing ones you wrote down. Engaging in this self-amplifying feedback loop of positivity and clarity will assist you in building a better brain with more positive and consciously clarified thoughts as a foundation for your thinking in general.

## Neuroscience Behind Our Existence

It's easy to go through life and not question the very "pictures" and "videos" your brain shows you. Existence is no more than neurons firing in your brain, taking in information from various sensors (like your ears and fingers) to then vividly create a reality you see in front of you like a projector screen. In reality, the information being displayed is not on a movie theater screen but the projector in the back playing mini-images with a combination of light and moving pictures.

You ever wonder why those pictures on Instagram of the different colored white and gold or blue and black sweater look different to each person? It's easy to dismiss these as an optical illusion, but the very word illusion can be a bigger analogy of the illusion of life's experience itself. That's because we are all very much not living in the same reality and our brains and other various biological processes are the ones running the show.

A study published in the *Journal of Research in Personality* found that your personality and mood can impact low level perceptual experiences correlated with the personality trait of being more open minded. Meaning, if you are more creative, you literally see the world in a visually different way.

Another study in *Progress in Brain Search* even found that practices like meditation (which we will cover in later chapters) influence our neurobiology, where processes like our perception itself, action, attention, and learning are coherently orchestrated, according to the single general mandate of free-energy minimization. This is just a way of saying that the energy you experience daily is how your brain processes information via your senses as well as your internal state, which can be regulated with meditation.

Have you ever heard of cognitive biases and distortions? According to leading researchers, our brains, through thousands of years, have created these mini-backdoors. These are like shortcuts to processing information, the same way a computer works. Instead of right clicking text on a document or website, hitting copy, then going to another document, right clicking and hitting paste, you can just hit CTRL + C, then CTRL + V. Our brain does the same thing, but life is not as simple as a computer. Our brain is a highly sophisticated growing meta computer that can be wrong in many ways. Science says there are anywhere between 65 to 175 cognitive distortions that make our reality work, but research may identify either fewer or more than anticipated.

According to a study out of Brooklyn by Benson (2016), cognitive biases help us address four different problems and filter down the over 100 biases into shortcuts or reasons for their place.

> Problem 1: Too much information to deal with (information overload): our brain uses tricks to select the information we are most likely to use.
> Problem 2: Not enough meaning; we need to make sense out of what we perceive. To solve this problem, we fill in the gaps.
> Problem 3: Need to act fast.
> Problem 4: What should we remember?

These meta problems that make up our life day to day and the functions of our brains can be a large contributor to an individual experiencing social anxiety. In fact, the study goes on to lay out the potential issues with each one of these distortions.

> Downside 1: We don't see everything. Some of the information we filter out is actually useful and important.
> Downside 2: Our search for meaning can conjure illusions. We sometimes imagine details that were filled in by our assumptions, and construct meaning and stories that aren't really there.
> Downside 3: Quick decisions can be seriously flawed. Some of the quick reactions and decisions we jump to are unfair, self-serving, and counter-productive.
> Downside 4: Our memory reinforces errors. Some of the stuff we remember for later just makes all of the above systems more biased, and more damaging to our thought processes.

Another researcher by the name of Duncan Pierce (n.d.) goes on to categorize the cognitive biases using the following groupings and the implications of daily life:

<u>Social and group effects:</u> Social and group related biases are biases primarily involving relationships with other people. These biases may be helpful in understanding group interactions in organizations.
<u>Attitude to risk and probability:</u> These biases affect how individual people makes decisions in the presence of uncertainty and risk, or with probabilistic outcomes. They may have an influence on planning and decision-making activities.
<u>Seeking/recognizing/remembering information:</u> The information we internalize can be strongly affected by our existing ideas. What stands out strongly to one person may not be noticed by another. There are several cognitive biases about attention–how we direct our noticing and evaluating activities.
<u>Evaluating information:</u> How we evaluate the information we are aware of can also be strongly affected by our existing ideas and some seemingly built-in thinking "shortcuts" we apply.
<u>Taking action:</u> Once the information is available and has been evaluated sufficiently to allow action to be taken, other cognitive biases may have an effect on the actions we take, perhaps delaying or prolonging them.
<u>Memory, retrospection:</u> Once action has been taken, the ways in which we evaluate the effectiveness of what we did may be biased, influencing our future decision-making.
<u>Judgment and liking:</u> How we judge others and expect them to judge us (in terms of liking, moral acceptability, etc.), may be influenced by a number of biases.

Now, I'm not saying that life is just a puppet show that someone is running from the inside of the mind. There are very real physical complications in the material world, but the way in which we act in the world, is based on a model that our brains created as an attempt to accurately model the world. However, life is very complicated. Add in each individual person (8 billion) trying to live their own life and how it intersects with other people's mental models of the world and you have a recipe for cognitive dissonance.

For example, I faced a tremendous amount of racism and bullying. My brain heard time and time and time again from others that I was a terrorist, or I was a sand n\*\*\*er, or I would never amount to anything and just be poor my entire life. Or maybe it was the fact that I *was* poor in a town where most people were not poor. Seeing my peers in the latest styles while I wore the same clothes day in and day out may have reinforced the thought that I was worthless.

Why? Because my values and mental models were set primarily on external wealth, and we all know money does not create happiness. But, in the example I just gave, my peers had great lives, but their mental models could be telling them that life sucks, their parents hate them, and they buy things to compensate for sadness. Unless we have authentic conversations, we don't know the truth behind others' realities. Yet, my brain and the mental model created from my experience and values does not accurately reflect the world, but reflects my mental model of the world and in turn shapes my behavior and actions.

This lack of awareness and religious embodiment of trusting everything my brain shows me with a healthy dose of skepticism sets the ideal breeding grounds for having poor mental health and not actually living the life you want to live. Now, I know everything I just said could be misunderstood or not understood at all unless you've lived it. It's hard to read a book with just the written word or if you're listening to this via audiobook and try to level up the fidelity of your experience.

A word you may or may not have heard of before that's important to understand before we move on is Serotonin. What is serotonin? A neurotransmitter that primarily rules the way in which we process information from the world. There are many other chemicals and elements that work in tandem to impact our perception of the world, but let's focus on serotonin for now.

**Serotonin**, synthesized from the amino acid tryptophan, is an important monoamine neurotransmitter in the brain and in the peripheral nervous system. Serotonin plays an important neuro-modulatory role in physiological responses; for example, behavioral arousal, circadian rhythmicity, neuroendocrine function, sexual behaviors, and feeding. Serotonin also plays an important role in mental processes, such as mood and cognition, and is implicated in many psychiatric disorders.

What's even more interesting is that a study from the *Journal of Psychiatry and Neuroscience* found four fundamental ways to increase serotonin without any drugs.

1. Alterations in thought, either self-induced or due to psychotherapy (measured via positron emission tomography)
2. Exposure to bright light
3. Exercise
4. Diet (Most of your serotonin isn't produced in the brain, but rather in the gut microbiome which we will discuss in the coming chapters)

In layman's terms, this means your thoughts (mindset), exposure to the sun (outside), your ability to move, and what you put in your mouth are the four primary modalities you can control to ultimately not just alleviate social anxiety but also other mental issues like depression. Yet, most of the world ignores these and attempts to pass the narrative that this is just the way you are when in reality you are experiencing an output based on underlying flawed biochemical processes happening in the brain. We will visit each one of these elements in the chapters to come and address how each person can create an actionable plan to tackle the elements.

**The moment I realized the experience of my reality is a biochemical equation, everything changed. I started to view my social anxiety as a science project I could work on rather than a moral failure I couldn't touch or change.**

## Truth Is the Chiropractor of the Mind

It doesn't matter if you take the best medicine, eat the best food, use the best exercise regiment, have the best friends, the best business, or the best significant other if you are not living in the alignment of your life's truth. Not living in the truth of your life enables you to distort the very elements that keep reality grounded. The Truth is defined as the structural foundation in which living happens while your values and what's important to you are properly aligned. If you are lying all the time to yourself and others, you cannot take any action in your day to day life meaningfully and see a return on your investment. You will feel like a fraud or imposter until you don't even recognize life anymore.

Let's take a look at an example of lying to oneself that most people don't recognize:

Let's say you are not the best student at school. You are sitting in your high school history classroom. The teacher asks the students if anyone knows when World War 1 happened? All of a sudden you remember from the documentary you watched last night that in 1914, WW1 started. Now, you get another thought from your brain that says, "Eh that's not right, you are a stupid person, remember?" You don't raise your hand, but another kid raises his hand and says 1914 and the teacher says, Bravo! You are so smart."

You just lied to yourself. You were confronted with two versions of yourself. One, the true one that gave you the answer. Another that insulted you and distorted the truth to get you to do something that you wouldn't normally do. Essentially, what just happened was you saw the real you, and you rejected him or her. Every time you do that, you take the fake, distorted version of yourself that has been created through lies and you bring him or her to the front in place of the real you. Know that every time you lie, you are shoving the real you more and more and more to the back of your life. Next thing you know, you don't even know who the real you is.

I lied so much to myself and others; I began living a fake life. A fake life I didn't even know was fake but highly distorted and not true to myself. The consequences of doing this time and time again is becoming unmotivated in your life. Not having the drive or pull to do anything at all except for the things you MUST do or have been doing on auto-pilot. This lack of motivation will cause you to grow apathetic towards your life, continuing to extend what first started as a fake distortion, but now you don't even feel your real emotions. You are not even doing what you want to do, not because you don't want to do those things deep down, but because of your lies, you have created a fake version of life. Next thing you know, you will surround yourself with other liars and institutions and programs not aligned with the truth either, which will continue to descend you down this crazy rabbit hole you don't know how to get out of. Welcome to Hell.

This is just like the classic fairy tale of *Pinnochio*. You know that crazy story with the wooden puppet that becomes a real boy whose crazy adventure eventually lands him in the belly of a whale in the middle of the ocean? Pinnochio is first made in the material world in the form of a wooden puppet. After his maker lays down in his bed, he smokes something in his pipe and then goes to his windowsill. He sees a shooting star and makes a wish that his wooden boy becomes real. In the middle of the night, a magical glowing fairy visits the puppet and makes him into a real boy meant to do good in this world. The next morning Pinnochio does in fact wake up real and his father is so overjoyed that they sing and dance together. Pinnochio meets his conscience, represented by a goofy looking Jiminy cricket, who gives him the introduction to life. He explains that in life sometimes what feels right, is actually wrong, and what feels wrong is sometimes actually right.

Pinnochio is sent off to school by his father after getting a brief pep talk on how life works. Pinnochio goes marching off in the street on his way to school and is quickly confronted by two cunning foxes dressed as fancy gentlemen. The foxes trick Pinnochio without much effort into becoming a puppet actor to achieve success and fame. All of a sudden his conscience wakes up late, realizes that Pinnochio is gone, and chases after him. This represents that our conscience awareness is usually late to the party and by the time Jiminy cricket gets to

Pinnochio to try to convince him not to go with strangers, the puppet has already made up his mind and goes with the foxes.

The next day, the same thing happens. Pinnochio meets two of the same foxes, who trick the boy again into meeting a much worse person portrayed as a big old guy who takes children to Pleasure Island. Advertised as the land of no rules, you can do anything you want to: drink, smoke as much as you want, and, to a teenage boy, considered the promised land. Pinnochio heads to the island with hundreds of other boys and all you see are people smoking, drinking, playing pool, destroying things, and intoxicated by pleasure. Pleasure Island represents the state of mind you enter when you don't care about anything in life, have no responsibility, and lack values or priorities.

I've been to Pleasure Island before; I call it College. Where many of us graduate high school and don't have the closest clue about what we should be doing with our lives. We are sent to this four year camp where we are assigned educational materials so we can learn and graduate into the real world. When I was in college, I realized that I indeed had no idea what I was doing with my life, and I didn't want to commit to studying something for four years that I didn't really care about. If you are in college and you realize this and don't have any experience, you might think it's the end of the world. No clear path before you, not following in the footsteps of your friends and family that told you to go on a specific path. So, it becomes easier to distract yourself than to pick up that sense of responsibility and do what you actually want to be doing. When I was on Pleasure Island, I ate, drank, smoked, gossiped, neglected, and resented my way to becoming unsuccessful, toxic, and nihilistic.

But here's the thing; in the film *Pinnochio,* as he and all his friends are drinking, eating, smoking, etc., they all begin to slowly turn into donkeys. When Pinnochio sees this happening, he freaks out and stops smoking, drinking, or doing anything on the island. What this represents is as you do the wrong behaviors, as you lie to yourself, the very structures of what you consider life, including yourself, change for the worse until you can't even recognize yourself. Pinnochio had to not just leave the island, but go to the bottom of the ocean and face a monster whale that tries to eat him and kill him. The puppet had to go to the very depths of his soul, to the bottom, to discover who he was and his purpose. He could have not jumped in the ocean, he could have tried to just glide by in life and live with his donkey ears and tails, undoubtedly making him into an even bigger donkey.

Although this story is not specifically about social anxiety, it can be a great pathway to understand how the human consciousness perceives reality and how it reacts to the moving pieces and obstacles. Do not lie. Do not take part in behaviors that are not true to who you are. Do not fall victim to the flashy rewards and false promises of success told to you by people who are also unsuccessful. The blind leading the blind is perhaps the fastest way to end up with a terrible life. Instead, find people who have the life you want and learn from them; model what they do and bring their traits that resonate with you into who you are.

**Exercise:** Sit down with a piece of paper. Make sure you are in an uninterrupted space for up to 30 to 45 minutes. That sounds like a lot of time, but trust me, this is going to be worth it if you take this seriously. Ask yourself the following questions.

1. What lies have I told recently?
2. Why did I tell those lies?
3. What lies have I told in the past?
4. What are my biggest deepest darkest secrets almost nobody knows about me?
5. Why have I ignored these lies or not been conscious of them before?
6. Did I hurt anybody other than myself with these lies?
7. Do I need to make any reparations?
8. How can I get myself to never lie to myself again?

If that wasn't motivating enough for you to take this social anxiety mission for yourself seriously, the chapter below is for you.

# 3.

# Life's Greatest Invention

Do you know what our greatest fear is of all time?

It's not talking to people.

It's not getting rejected.

It's not getting hurt.

It's not living alone and having no friends.

It's not even our loved ones being sad or in pain.

The biggest fear to the human psyche is death, that we will perish one day and what exists in front of us will no longer be available. It's easy to dismiss what you just read as stupid maybe because you've never thought of it from this perspective before. You might think to yourself, yea death isn't a great thing, but it's certainly not my top fear. Here's the thing: why do you think every single major culture, religion, and community on planet earth has thoughts on the afterlife?

Whether it's Christianity's heaven and hell, or Hindu's belief in reincarnation, every well-established community has created a solution for this undeniable element of life. When you are born into a society where this fact has already been established, you may never even think about it and take it as a given, regardless if the solution is right or wrong. And if you haven't thought of it before, you may have a very deep sense of fear that you have allowed into your conscious mind, yet it is still lingering and processing in the background.

I don't have anything negative to say about any religion, but having other people think for you, especially generations and generations of people's thinking passed down, is a recipe for a life filled with unconscious fear, dread, and confusion. We can learn from ancient traditions, cultures, and perhaps try to assimilate some timeless wisdom into our own lives. For example, in the Christian belief system, depending on which denomination and individual you speak to, if you do something wrong and don't repent, you will go to hell. This is not good. Why? Because as humans, we have evolved to have vivid imaginations that help us create a future reality in our minds, which then enables us to do stuff in the present moment because we have hope there will be a better tomorrow.

If you are stuck thinking that because you did something wrong, there is something inherently wrong with you, and you will burn not just in your life here on earth, but FOREVER and EVER in a land where time doesn't exist, that's so painful for your soul it's hard to describe. I have chosen to not believe in hell.

I believe in a hell, but just as a state of mind because I've been there before. I'm not talking about living a life without consequences either. I'm talking about living your own life with keeping the highest values of truth, love, responsibility, self-growth, and being of service to others. In fact, Jesus himself has repeatedly stated that forgiveness and love are the doorways out of "hell" and into eternal love. For you non-religious folk out there, take everything I just said non-religiously. I am speaking about the history of humanity and the ideas we have thought that enabled our society to exist, fall down, rebuild, be invaded, get conquered, re-build, and introduce new ideas.

If you are an unconscious individual and try your best to not think about big ideas or yourself in the greater context of the world and existence, you may have never thought about this before and may have never found this out until you are on your deathbed. But odds are, if you are reading this book, that's not you. You need to address your deep psychological beliefs that you may have never thought of before in your life. You need to live with the belief that one day you will die, and everything and everyone you do cherish, and value, will be gone. This doesn't mean you need to fear death at all but come to terms with it.

I am not afraid of death. Well, at least I'm not now in this moment while writing this book. To me, death is another stage of life where my body and mind will be reunited with my spirit and soul and continue living on in another dimension that I can't comprehend. I'll figure it out when I get there, but I'm not afraid of death. Once upon a time I used to be. I used to fear death in the sense of, if I were to die right now, would I have any regrets? Back then, when I wasn't living my own life, and if I had died, I would have had so many regrets; my soul might as well have been sent to hell due to the anxiety and mental anguish.

The reason why I've included a chapter on death in this book is this is perhaps your biggest reason for doing what you do. If you really understand that you will die one day, are you going to fear the opinions (which are neurotransmitters firing together in your brain) of other people when you want to do what you want to do? Are you really going to fear picking up the phone and calling up somebody and telling them what you have always wanted to tell them if you know we're all going to die one day? Are you really going to be shy and not participate and speak up and add valuable thought and value to others?

**I was first introduced to this idea when I heard Steve Jobs famously say: "Death is very likely the single best invention of life. Your time is limited, so don't waste it living somebody else's life."**

When I heard this in my college dorm room in 2016, it completely changed my life. I grew up in a Christian household, and as much as I don't like labels, I still consider myself a Christian (because of the great meta-morals and values it teaches). but, I never ever consciously thought of my own death. When I slowly began to come to terms with the fact that I could step outside of my apartment and get hit by a truck and die, I began asking myself: Why the hell would I care about perceived opinions of what I do in my life? Why the hell wouldn't I have done what I wanted to for the sake of my own life, the people I love, and the future of this world?

Am I really going to avoid doing what I want to do deep down when I know either way I'm going to end up in a graveyard somewhere? Reminding yourself you are going to die is not only the best invention of life but is also the deepest sense of motivation that exists on planet earth. It is paramount to anyone finding a reason to reinvent and change their life. I interviewed Mark Manson, mega best-selling author of *The Subtle Art of Not Giving a F*ck*, and he mentioned this really interesting point about something he calls "Immortality Projects". This idea that if we know we are going to die one day, we're going to invest our time and resources into something that will still be here on earth even after we die. Like a statue, foundation, company, book, painting, music, etc., that will still be a piece of us left once we perish. Working on an immortality project decreases your overall anxiety on death and what you will leave behind that will be here past your mortal body.

Lifespan is expanding more and more now than ever. If you take care of your health, some longevity experts like Dave Asprey, founder of *Bulletproof*, say you could live to 150. Once you get to 150, who knows what kind of technology could exist to make us live even longer. Immortality may or may never be possible with technology, but that's beside the point. I included this chapter in the book because I believe death is the ultimate motivator, like Steve Jobs said to get you off your butt and to understand the very real consequences of doing or not doing what you want to do with your life. It's easy to dismiss this rationally in your logical mind, but one must think about this every single day.

Personally, on the days I remember I take out my journal or some other writing device like an iPad, I write an oath to myself. Almost like the frontside of my tombstone that states why I'm even getting up in the morning in the first place. It can be easy to get up and do what you have to do to feed your family or to survive war, but that largely isn't a big factor in the world we live in today. If you have some sort of wealth, where you can survive by going to work for a portion of the day, never think about where your next meal is coming from, and the biggest dangers are your kids crossing the street, it can be hard to get up and actually live your own life, as crazy as it seems.

When I write down the legacy I want to create, it extends my line of thinking past my own selfish little existence and enables me to integrate myself and the change I want to accomplish into the world. Even then, if you write this every morning, usually by 3 or 4 in the afternoon, you are tired and begin to slowly wean into the behaviors you don't want to be doing due to lack of energy and a disconnection of your attentive purpose. I began seeing this in myself and decided to utilize technology to help remind me.

On my iPhone, I set a reminder that's one of the few notifications that go off and states "You're Gonna Die One Day!!!" twice. Once at 9am and another one at 3pm. If you have never heard of this, it may seem pointless or stupid or that it can't possibly work. It's not my magic pill, but as I'm going throughout my busy life and I get this notification, I have seen it shift my state of mind. Sometimes I'll be at back to back meetings that I don't want to do and might feel some sense of dread or laziness. Then I'll get this reminder on my phone and all of sudden, my mind starts looking at the big picture.

If this is the last meeting or point of communication with this purpose, what do I want to get across to them? Will they come to my funeral for a deep real human sense of meaning? What can I do to help this person in my final days here on planet earth?

If you are an entrepreneur like me, there's massive talk on the importance of focus. A friend of mine, Sharran Srivatsaa, CEO of a real estate company worth $3.4 billion says, "Focus is more important than intelligence. Relentless focus is what will get you to your destination day in and day out." However, there's also a big problem with focus. If you focus on something time and time and time again, you will always find a problem with it. Over focusing can lead to mental health issues like obsessive compulsive disorder, and trying to think a thought so profound for so long eventually cripples you. I know this might seem counterintuitive to what you have heard, but sometimes you need to look at the big picture. Sometimes you need to stop looking at what's in front of you right now and instead focus on the macro, your life's legacy that will make undergoing the pains of existence worth it.

## Death's Greatest Takeaway

But here's the biggest catch with death. Cognitively knowing that you will perish one day forces you to take responsibility for who you are in each and every moment. Some people in the minority have a distorted sense of too much responsibility for who they are but most of us are far from that and try our best to never take responsibility. When was the last time you took responsibility for something bad that happened in your life? When was the last time you took responsibility over every single thing that's happened in your life? I'm saying everything.

**As Will Smith notes, most people confuse the words responsibility with fault.**

**It's not your fault your parents got divorced.**

**It's not your fault everyone hates you at school.**

**It's not your fault when you were 7 years old you were sexually molested.**

**It's not your fault that your uncle and mom died in a car accident 3 years ago.**

**But, it is your responsibility.**

**You are responsible for how you feel now because your parents got divorced.**

**You are responsible that everyone used to hate you at school.**

**You are responsible for the person who was created because at 7 years old you were sexually molested.**

**You are responsible for who you are today because your uncle and mom died in a car accident 3 years ago.**

**Responsible = Response Able**

**The ability to <u>make a decision</u> and choose to act**

Taking responsibility for all the good and bad that's happened in your life is where all of your true innate power lies. You are now able to choose your response because you have taken responsibility over your life; therefore, you can now change what's in your life. Most people never get this far. Most people are still cursing their past selves because they have never forgotten nor loved who they were prior, which is actually you because time is an illusion. Most people are still resentful because their parents treated them in a way that changed their lives - maybe for the worse. Most people are still conspiring and cursing towards the sky at the government, maybe a god, or a corporation as to why their life sucks. All of these people have created the belief that something on the outside has changed who they are on the inside.

Again, don't get me wrong. Terrible life experiences can occur for no apparent reason, but don't associate fault versus responsibility as we mentioned before, because at the end of the day, you blame something outside of you and now you have detached responsibility from your life. How can you control something you don't own?

Which means, you are unable to respond to life's events as your authentic self and get stuck in the same repetitive loops of behavior, also known as frozen in a grey bubble of time where the same events and feelings repeat themselves again and again. Welcome to the Matrix. Most people attempt to escape this with impulsive pleasures that can give them a moment of feeling great, like eating a treat or smoking something in attempt to flee the deep abyss of an un-comfortable and cold reality with no meaning.

This is where I lived for most of my life. I listened to all of the mainstream 21st century advice of trying to do the easiest thing possible, relax and comfort yourself whenever possible, and choose temporary short term pleasures over challenging ventures that will provide me a more meaningful, longer lasting, deeper sense of happiness and fulfillment. I listened to perceived authority figures, brightly colored TV commercials, and the well intentioned people around me to always take the easy way out, but that makes life not as challenging and therefore not as enjoyable.

Imagine playing a first person shooter zombie video game where the main objective is to kill a ton of zombies. You're in the game, you've got your weapon, but there are no zombies around you at all. Would that be fun? Absolutely not. That's also what life is like for us. Would life even be meaningful if there were no challenges we had to take responsibility for? Nope. It's almost as if once you take responsibility for all the good and bad of your life, and accept what life is, you are given a controller now because you get how the rules work.

If you understand everything I just told you, and still find a way somehow to not do anything with your life. Your anxiety will get worse. To recap, so far we've talked about how social anxiety isn't actually your main problem and there are deeper things going on below the surface issues. We've talked about the true reality of our existence when it comes to communicating with others, neurochemistry, and how important the truth is, as well as death being one of the main motivators of life. Let's say you're sitting here, and you've read this book to this point and you're thinking to yourself, "Mark, that's great and all, but I am still lazy and have no energy to do what I want to do."

I want to make something very clear: there is a big difference between your mind not wanting to do something, and your body not wanting to do something. Growing up, I certainly lacked in my mental abilities, but I believe I was gifted with my thinking. I tremendously lacked in my physical body of not wanting to do anything. Why? Not because I was unmotivated but because I had no energy. We will discuss this differentiation in the next chapter and how it is a critical aspect of dealing with being shy and social anxiety that not many people touch on.

**Exercise:** Again, find time where you can sit down with yourself uninterrupted and write out your tombstone. Write down what legacy you want to be known for when you are dead and gone. Imagine what other people feel or say about you because of the impact you created. Write a list of everything you are responsible for in your life, including past events, priorities, things you did, etc.

# 4.

# Biochemistry Your Biggest Starting Leverage Point

Remember that scene at the beginning of this book? Sitting at a restaurant with my sister and somehow being able to talk to a waitress without a sweat for the first time in my life. You know how that happened? Not because I decided to go out on a massive journey to eliminate my anxiety. But in fact, because I accidentally began to eat healthy over a period of months and lost weight. My diet always consisted of cookies, milk, cupcakes, chicken nuggets, etc., and when I switched, my mind became clear for the first time in my life.

When I talk about physiology in my day to day life, almost everyone ignores me. Almost every single person I talk to about the BIGGEST leverage point in social anxiety and overall human performance is physiology, yet they ignore it. Most people ignore this because it's easy to logically accept these points in your brain and not change your behavior rather than drop the box of Twinkie's and stop sitting down for four hours at a time.

Food is the world's greatest addiction. Growing up, I never experimented with drugs and alcohol but abused food as an anti-anxiety medication. If you are addicted to drugs, for example, and you go to rehab and eventually get clean, that's one thing. But, being addicted to food and trying to get clean is much more difficult because you have to eat every single day. I remember I would eat when

I was nervous, scared, unsure, angry, bored, hesitant, and I usually didn't binge on broccoli - Oreos at 2 o'clock in the morning were my thing.

I eat healthy, sleep 7-8 hours each night, and exercise every single day to improve my mental health. To be quite honest, I'm not even interested in my physical health or how I look other than the fact that physical health is heavily correlated to mental health. So, if you're reading this and are very shy and 300 pounds, you have a bright shining indicator right there of what you need to work on. However, most people approach this in the wrong way. Let's say you're not 300 pounds and you're skinny or average weight for your height and age and think you can ignore this chapter. Nope! If anything, average looking people from the outside can suffer from more problems internally than people with seemingly poor physical health.

I did not know that food could impact your life other than how much you weigh. It was particularly eye opening to see that the *American Journal of Public Health* released a systematic study showing evidence of a significant, cross-sectional relationship between unhealthy dietary patterns and poorer mental health in children and adolescents. I was especially intrigued to see another study by BMC Medicine which found that adults who eat a western processed diet are at risk for a smaller hippocampus. Do you know what that part of your brain even does? The hippocampus regulates motivation, emotion, learning, and memory. If that is not a major red flag for someone's state of mental health and their state of mind in general, I don't know what is.

## First My Gut Broke, Then My Brain Broke

I want to take you back to my journey, my story when I was sitting in my college dorm room and I had gained not the freshman 15, but the freshman 60. At one point in my life, I was over 220 pounds, never having gained a serious amount of weight in my life prior to this time. Why? Because I was depressed and was using food as a coping mechanism. I felt a massive hole in my soul that I tried to fill with candy, pizzas, sandwiches, chicken wings - really whatever I could get my hands on that would drug my brain with pleasure for 10 minutes. I would wake up tired, and then do the same thing over and over again in a vicious cycle to try and give myself energy and happiness. This is a broken cycle. In fact, the World Health Organization reports that diseases like obesity, diabetes, cardiovascular disease, cancer, osteoporosis, and dental diseases are predominantly caused due to an individual's choice of diet.

Guess what happened? I got even more depressed, way MORE socially anxious, and began to socially isolate myself. At one point, I even became suicidal. I'm not saying this all because of what I was doing to my body and brain with chemicals, but a large part of continuing this pattern of behavior enforced by the body. I was slowly beginning to realize that I had created a version of myself in the last 18 years of my life that I didn't want to be anymore. But there was such a big gap between who I was and who I wanted to be. Food wasn't even on my radar but doing big meaningful things in the world was; instead, I was sitting in a classroom paying tens of thousands of dollars to learn how to write AI code. So, there was a much bigger issue in my life that I was trying to mask or run away from. I was wasting my time with too much food, Netflix, and not living my own life. I was trying to escape rather than deal with the facts, make a plan, and adjust my behavior accordingly.

My initial breaking point came from not being able to sleep. I guess the 6 energy drinks I was chugging a day weren't helping. Neither was my incessant, anxious mind coming up with every possible scenario on how I could fail hitting me non-stop. In the next section, we will discuss what exactly to do about your sleep.

Unknowingly, what I began to do was go for walks at 1am. Guess what shifts your physiology? Moving! I initially went for these walks not trying to shift my body or brain because I was in so much emotional pain I wanted it to end. The solution I came up with was trying to walk in bad areas in my neighborhood so somebody would come and end my life. I never imagined myself taking my own life but would have definitely classified myself as suicidal but it's much easier to convince yourself that's the best solution when you are hopeless and helpless.

Next, I had this moment where I looked at myself in the mirror after I tried putting on a pair of pants and they didn't fit. I made direct eye contact with myself and just asked who am I and who am I becoming? At this time, I wasn't consciously aware of the fact that I was at my version of rock bottom. I wasn't even aware that I was depressed or socially isolating myself or any issue relating to mental health. So, I slowly but surely began a mission to tackle the most superficial layer of life I could perceive: physical reality and my body. Over the summer of 2016, I went on a crazy learning adventure trying to learn everything about losing weight, like the right kind of diet, exercise, and the biochemical foundations that make up our life, in an attempt to fix what I had unconsciously created.

I eventually went down a massive rabbit hole of what the heck am I supposed to eat? Vegan, Paleo, Plant-based, Carnivore, Pescatarian - and then I would stumble on an idea that states the food you eat doesn't matter because it's about counting calories! Or maybe eat 6 meals or day or do intermittent fasting and eat twice a day...I got cognitively destroyed and confused by the internet's inflating and complexity from the health and wellness industry. I got to the point where I was so desperate, I was willing to try anything. I tried going 100% plant based for 2 weeks; I felt great for a short while, and then felt like I had even less energy and more mood swings. I researched and researched and found a meta-analysis study out of Cornell University that showed a tight correlation between vegetarianism and increased rates of depression. In fact, the study analyzed a combined total of over 131,000 subjects and found this statement to be true. You can be plant-based, just make sure you are doing it right, with help from the right experts who rely on science and facts, not in getting people to believe in an ideology.

One day I was reading some random article online and saw a Google advert for putting butter and a form of coconut oil called MCT in your coffee, also known as Bulletproof coffee. The first thing that popped into my head was this is complete and utter BS. Butter is bad for you. Now you want me to put butter in my coffee? Screw it. I ordered it and told myself I'm just going to test this because there's no way it works. One week later, my coffee and MCT oil arrived. I went down to the grocery store and bought some Grass fed butter. I blended the coffee and drank it. Wow, that's delicious!

An hour later I felt energized, which never ever has happened with me drinking coffee. Usually when I would drink coffee, I would feel some sort of a head high for 15 minutes, and then it would disappear into a cloud of my fast paced thoughts and confusion. That didn't happen this time. In fact, I felt like myself. I had energy for several hours. Absolutely dumbfounded, I began to do more research on bulletproof and its creator Dave Asprey. Out of another moment of desperation, I bought the *Bulletproof Diet Recipe* on Amazon that explains a bit about the science behind nutrition as well as yummy food creations you can prepare with minimal effort but with all the nutritional benefits.

The book arrived. I remember sitting in my college dorm room bed reading this book and going through each chapter understanding different nutritional elements like hormones, biochemical signals, and how they impact how we think on a moment to moment basis. Nobody in my life had ever told me that food is more about your waistline, but the actual quality of your thoughts in your brain are also part of the diet. I never gained clarity that the thoughts in my brain were causing my social anxiety because I always had brain fog. Why? Because my biochemical system wasn't working properly, and food is the biggest leverage point you have against that. You are what you eat!

Now, I'm not saying you have social anxiety because you don't eat well, but it might well be your biggest leverage point. Why? Because social anxiety is so hard to get out of and tackling the first physical physiological layer is the easiest. This book will go through the layers we need to go through to eliminate social anxiety, but I remember in my journey, I couldn't even fathom talking to somebody until I began to gain the energy and mental clarity from a proper diet. So, this is not the be all, end all of facing social anxiety, but it's one of the first layers we can tackle to begin the journey.

**You can't run good software on poor hardware. Doesn't matter how much you try. It's like trying to install iOS 13 on the iPhone 3.**

## A Strong Mind Is Built in the Kitchen

Never in my life growing up had I ever heard someone tell me the kinds of food you eat will probably be in the top 5 of the most important decisions of your entire life. I always thought if you ate too much food, you would gain weight. That's all. In this chapter, I will be speaking on nutrition and its association with mental health. To be honest, I have almost no interest in physical health, although science tells us good physical health = good mental health. However, I did lose over 65 pounds and starting this year, I am lifting weights and have already gained almost 20 pounds in muscle. If you were also once like me, you probably don't know the correlation between what you put in your mouth and the way your brain thinks.

My evolution with food has transformed over the years. Originally, when I set out on this journey of life, as a kid I would eat chocolate chip cookies, chocolate milk, fried chicken fingers, fries, and other yummy but low nutrition value foods. Oh, and very rarely would I drink water; I'd just chug soda, fruit juices, and energy drinks. When I got into this groove of losing weight with the Bulletproof diet, it became a version of the ketogenic diet, which primarily relies on dietary fat, so foods like avocados, eggs, pumpkin seeds, salmon, ribeye steaks, olive oil, etc. Today, I am not keto but eat a general whole foods diet with an emphasis on fat from the things that come from the ground or have been walking or swimming around, and last time I checked, chips and soda don't come from the ground unless you drop your bag of chips on the floor and believe in the 5 second rule.

Everyone is at a different point on their health journey. Some of you may have been eating healthy and exercising for years, while others may have never eaten anything green in your life other than Christmas sugar cookies. No matter what, it's all good because you are now becoming conscious of this universal fact that our mental health is so heavily connected with our diet; it's honestly scary. And hey it's not just mental health; a Bill and Melinda Gates study found in our modern world, the #1 cause of death from chronic disease is processed food, frequent alcohol consumption, and over consumption of soda. If I haven't scared you enough, perhaps you should ask the 65% of Americans who are obese and have levels of depression and anxiety and are stuck in the relentless, brutal cycle I used to live in.

This is not random. The food you eat goes to every single one of your cells. Imagine trying to feed a supercar with not fuel but Oreo's and coca cola and expecting it to drive normally. If your body doesn't recognize an ingredient, cellular dysfunction occurs, which may have ranging symptoms from spiraling thoughts of anxiety, to a skin rash, to not being able to sleep all night, which in turn all impact your mental health. I'll be the first one to tell you I don't have a 100% clean diet by choice. But 99% of the time what I eat is clean, and I consider myself in an excellent spot mentally. However, if I go off on a bender eating a ton of junk food for a full day or more, I will be tired, I will be depressed, I will be more anxious than usual because that's how my body and brain work.

This is my methodology for helping somebody get their food right.

1. Do not focus on NOT eating junk food. Focus on finding ways to just insert veggies, fiber and fats into your diet.
2. Wean off sugar (the biggest anxiety drug out there) by substituting other forms of sugar temporarily (Fructose from fruit is the best temporary option) and over time, reduce quantities.
3. Food is not about getting five minutes of tasting pleasure. You are what you eat. It's not about getting fat; this is about your mental health, what kind of performance you are willing to bring to this playing field of life, and how you love yourself.
4. Every bite you take is either bringing you closer to health and longevity or disease and dysfunction.
5. Environment is extremely important for initially regulating what you eat.

For those just starting out on your journey, evaluate what you are eating. Until discovering the facts I mentioned above, you may not even be aware of what you have been eating. Maybe your parents cook, or you always eat out. For example, for breakfast you eat some cereal with milk, as a snack you eat some trail mix, lunch you eat a turkey sandwich with chips, snack you eat a granola bar, and for dinner you sit down with a good friend of yours and eat spaghetti with meatballs At the end of the night, you head home super tired but remember you have a half pint of double fudge ice cream waiting for you in your freezer and can't wait.

Here's what I would do differently to optimize a diet for mental performance and health.

What if next to your cereal and milk for breakfast you eat a couple eggs or half a delicious avocado? Or you could even substitute your cereal with Magic Spoon, a *TIME* magazine 2019 top invention of the year healthy alternative made with no sugar but tastes the same if not better than brightly colored supermarket cereal.

What if within your trail mix you add in some natural almonds, pumpkin seeds, and walnuts, and take out the candies or fruits? Or better yet, what if you tried to make your own trail mix with no added sugar but just the natural ingredients you love eating?

What if inside your turkey sandwich with mayo you add some wild arugula, and that other half of your avocado? Better yet, what if you substituted that plain white bread with some whole sprouted grain bread with no added sugar, preservatives, or chemicals?

What if instead of eating the same granola bar that's filled with caramel and chocolate and has 32 grams of sugar, you try to find a healthier version of a granola or protein bar that tastes just as great if not better and doesn't make you feel like crap after? It can be tricky to find the right kind of bar however, as most are laden with chemicals and preservatives. My best rule of thumb is when I flip the package over and look at the ingredients, if I can't recognize something, my body won't either. Natural foods are the ingredients themselves and not chemicals pepto-dehydrated dioxide titanium.

What if instead of eating fried chicken wings you eat some baked wings? Make them together with a friend at home in your oven and now you have a group activity too!

What will begin to happen slowly is as you begin to give your body and brain nutrients, fiber, and good dietary fat, you will get fuller and feel a bit better, not rely on junk food, and avoid binges at the end of the day where you are still feeling hungry. As you continue to do this, you will notice your body isn't as pulled to that chocolate bar or that cheeseburger as usual. When you're not as pulled to those choices at a biological level, you will begin to regain control over your food decisions and not feel like you are in a constant battle.

Everyone is different. Some people have been eating only junk food for most of their lives, like myself. This process may take you a few months to a year to complete and adapt to. But, the common rule to understand is that the more natural, healthy food you can add to your diet, the less your body will crave these harmful artificial chemicals in most of our food supply today.

In fact, a study from the University of Michigan found that highly processed foods, which may share characteristics with drugs of abuse (e.g. high dose, rapid rate of absorption) appear to be particularly associated with food addiction. This means that junk food literally makes your brain crave the unhealthy ingredients and become addicted. This means that a processed food company, whose CEO probably makes tens of millions of dollars is using your body as a vessel to profit and make money, is in turn creating disease and dissatisfaction in you.

If you asked me what the ideal diet is for me, it's this - and it definitely changes from time to time as there's no such thing as a universal healthy diet.

**Breakfast**: Omelet with some kale and sometimes I'll throw in an onion and avocado on the side if I'm feeling it, doused in extra virgin olive oil.

**Lunch**: Big salad with wild arugula, pumpkin seeds, lemon, pickled onions, olives, olive oil, and a can of wild caught sardines on top of it. Mix it up, and it's one of the most delicious salads you'll ever eat. If you have never eaten sardines before, give them a try. Many people confuse them for their salty cousin, anchovies, and vow to never take a bite, but you might be surprised how delicious they are if you try. Also, make sure that your sardines are from a quality source and don't include any kind of toxic oils like canola.

**Dinner**: assorted roasted vegetables like sweet potato, brussels sprouts, broccoli, etc., and a piece of fat like grilled fish or a steak. Depending on the season, and if I'm trying to gain weight (which I am right now as I'm writing this book), I'll properly prepare some brown rice, lentils, or chickpeas doused in extra virgin olive oil.

Another hack I've found to deliver a ton of nutrients to my body in a simple, easily digestible way, is making a big nutrition shake in the middle of the day. Note that if you are consuming some of these ingredients for the first time, take it slow, and don't drink the entire thing quickly for the sake of fiber.

## Massive Nutrition Shake

I use a Ninja blender that chops up everything nicely:

- Celery

- Cucumber
- Lemon
- Frozen Spinach
- Frozen Raspberries
- Avocado
- Coconut Milk
- Hemp + Chia + Flax seeds
- Nut Butter (without added sugar or oil)

You are free to experiment with your own creation. I can make a shake in just 5 minutes and have a decent amount of nutrition and sustenance until I eat next. As of this writing, I'm strength training and growing my body, so I need to eat more. I might increase quantities in the shake to get more calories or fruit, but if you are trying to lose weight, I do not recommend making a massive shake but maybe a micro shake.

## 10 Key Minerals to Reduce Social Anxiety

If you just spent the last 18 years eating mostly terrible food like I have, you might need some extra firepower to give you that additional boost. On my journey, I began researching any critical minerals or compounds that could assist in rebuilding my brain. Luckily for me, I had already discovered Dave Asprey, the father of Bio-Hacking and founder of Bulletproof, who speaks extensively on supplements. I've had the honor of interviewing Dave not once, but twice, on my top 100 Humans 2.0 podcast, to get that direct information from him. Below are key minerals backed by science that will help you decrease anxiety at a biochemical level. Keep in mind that everyone's body is different and there is no such thing as universal truths. You will have to experiment for yourself to find the right combination.

The following chemical compounds are ranked in no particular order; they are simply the best choices for feeding your brain the right nutrients.

### *Omega 3 Essential Fatty Acids*

I'm sure you have already heard of Omega Fatty Acids. Did you know that the term Omega in biblical times is often a term to refer to God? Wow. If there's a chemical compound that has its roots with God, you can bet it's important. A study done by the Department of Child and Adolescent Psychiatry, Medical

University of Vienna in Austria, found that in those who take Omega 3's reduce the risk of progression to a psychotic disorder and may offer a safe and efficient strategy for indicated prevention in young people with subthreshold psychotic state and those who want to prevent these potential diseases. Another study from the Depression Clinical and Research Program, Massachusetts General Hospital and Harvard Medical School found a vital role in Omega-3 fatty acids in psychiatry, primarily in mood disorders, but also in psychotic disorders, attention-deficit disorder, obsessive-compulsive disorder, and personality disorders.

**Best Forms of All Omega Fatty Acids:**

- ALA (alpha-linolenic acid)
    - Flax, chia, and Hemp seeds
    - Walnuts and other seeds
    - Kale and Spinach
- EPA and DHA (eicosapentaenoic acid and docosahexaenoic acid)
    - Fish Oil
    - Herring
    - Salmon
    - Algae
    - Grass Fed Beef

*Vitamin D*
Although this book is about social anxiety, I've learned that many other health conditions are correlated alongside mental health. The moment when I began to consume quality food with high levels of bioavailable vitamin D, I watched my entire life change. Not only did I have more energy, but my asthma, skin rashes, and brain fog literally went away overnight, confirmed by my lab test results. I've found many credible studies that show correlation between low vitamin D status with a range of adverse neuropsychiatric outcomes. You can take a look at the studies in-depth at the end of this book under references.

Additionally, we live in an extremely, digitally connected world that has brought us plenty of prosperity, it also makes going outside much harder than just staying inside and playing video-games, watching tv shows, and scrolling through social media.

**Best Forms of Vitamin D:**

- Direct Sunlight Exposure
- The freshest wild caught seafood including salmon, mackerel, sardines.
- Beef Liver
- Mushrooms (Plant-based folk, focus on this hard!)
- Egg Yolks

If you do not eat the foods listed above, it may be best to take a quality Vitamin D supplement. If you are not sure on how much vitamin D you are getting, you can get tested to find out if you are deficient or overdoing it.

*Potassium*

Potassium is debatably the most important electrolyte that is involved in many cell functions all throughout our body. A study done by the School of Exercise and Nutrition Sciences found that dietary electrolytes like potassium are connected to our moment to moment mood.

**Best Forms of Potassium:**

- Sweet Potatoes and Potatoes
- Leafy Vegetables like Beet Greens and Spinach
- Avocados
- Lima Beans
- Salmon (superfood)
- Squash
- Brussel Sprouts
- Bananas

*Tryptophan*

Ah, the beloved serotonin precursor that is often associated with Thanksgiving turkey coma. Tryptophan will not make you sleepy but rather eating too much protein combined with sugars alongside your meal will put you to bed early. But, this is a key amino acid to digest in order for your body to generate serotonin and melatonin in your gut microbiome. In fact, there have been studies done that show tryptophan levels associated with participants who have panic attacks can have a protective effect on overall anxiety.

**Best Forms of Tryptophan:**

- Salmon
- Turkey and other forms of poultry
- Eggs
- Spinach
- Seeds and Nuts
- Watermelon
- Bananas

*Vitamin B1*

Vitamin B1 is debatably the most effective compound for treating rushing anxious thoughts. Why? Because depending on your blood glucose level, which is based off what you have been eating, you can potentially experience a drop if you eat foods filled with sugar and junk. Drops in blood sugar are correlated with no energy and anxiety. A study done by University of Saskatchewan College of Medicine observed irritability and mood problems in people known to be deficient in the B vitamins, as well as reported positive improvements in mental illness when treated with such nutrients.

**Best Forms of Vitamin B1:**

- Pork
- Asparagas
- Mussels
- Sunflower and Flaxseeds
- Beef
- Black Beans

*Vitamin B12*

The *Journal of Biomedical and Clinical Research* found remarkable results in a study:

"The correlation between depression and Vitamin B12 deficiency is an actual problem because it is a common condition with serious medical, social, and financial consequences and a poor prognosis. Vitamin B12 was found to be an effective option for treatment and prophylaxis of depression/anxiety."

**Best Forms of Vitamin B12:**

- Clams
- Beef Liver
- Nutritional Yeast
- Salmon, Trout, and Tuna
- Quality B12 Supplement

## *Vitamin B3*

Deficiency of Vitamin B3 has been linked to memory loss and mental confusion, fatigue, depression, headaches, diarrhea, and skin problems. These are all issues I used to suffer from, which would in turn make my social anxiety more of a jumbled mess that I couldn't sort through. In fact, a study from the Centre for Psychiatry Research and Department of Clinical Neuroscience in Stockholm, Sweden found that patients experiencing anxiety, depression, and even bipolar disorder that supplemented with Vitamin B3, or niacin, were stable and in a good mental health condition for up to 11 years without any pharmacologic interventions.

**Best Forms of Vitamin B3:**

- Chicken Breast
- Beef Liver
- Tuna
- Salmon
- Peanuts
- Avocados
- Lentils
- Brown Rice

## *Magnesium*

Magnesium is a supplement that has honestly changed my life. I experience such a vivid difference when I take it via a supplement or eat magnesium rich foods. If I feel anxious in the morning, I will take a quality magnesium supplement. But, if I don't I'll just take one at night before I go to bed because it has shown to impact sleep. A study from the University of Innsbruck in Austria found that deficiency in Magnesium has been linked to inducing anxiety.

**Best Forms of Magnesium:**

- Dark Chocolate (Get the highest % of cacao with 0 sugar)
- Avocados
- Almonds, Cashews, and Brazil Nuts
- Lentils, beans, and chickpeas
- Flax, Pumpkin, and Chia Seeds
- Kale, Spinach, Collard Greens, Turnip Greens, and Mustard Greens.

*Curcumin*

A study from the Department of Integrative Biology and Physiology at the University of California found that curcumin enhances the biosynthesis of hepatic DHA from n-3 precursors and enhances of the rate of growth DHA accretion in the brain. The data provided in the study shows a potential mechanism in which curcumin helps neurocognitive diseases like anxiety, Alzheimer's disease, major depressive disorder, schizophrenia with psychosis and impaired attention.

**Best Forms of Curcumin:**

- Turmeric

*Probiotics*

A joint study from the College of William and Mary, Department of Psychology and the University of Maryland found that for those high in neuroticism, eating more fermented food was associated with fewer symptoms of social anxiety. Taken together with previous studies, the results suggest that fermented foods that contain probiotics may have a protective effect against social anxiety symptoms.

**Best Forms of Probiotics:**

- Whole Fat Yogurt
- Kefir
- Sauerkraut
- Kimchi
- Kombucha
- Pickles (without Vinegar)

Please don't go out there any buy 10 of the most expensive supplements you can find. Eating food with these minerals and nutrients is ideally the best option for your body, but some of you may require higher doses to supplement. Personally, I supplement with fish oil, vitamin D, vitamin B12, and magnesium. The rest I can usually get from my diet. Try each one of these supplements out and reflect on how you feel from a moment to moment basis to analyzing your behavior by day and week to find out if these are effective for you.

At the end of the day, each one of these compounds have been unconsciously utilized for thousands of years by the healthiest humans who had a healthy diet that had all the right minerals and nutrients to properly fuel your brain and body for what you want to do in life.

## Rest and Intelligent Exponential Technology

*stomach growling*
Oh god.
*Rushes to the bathroom*

In 2018, I was working so hard on my business, podcast, life, and relationships that I slowly began to neglect self-improvement practices that help me deal with life better. I remember one day I was cooking lunch for myself, which was a salmon salad. It was the same thing I usually eat with assorted toppings like olives, avocados, pumpkin seeds, and olive oil. All of a sudden, my stomach started hurting in a way that it hadn't hurt in years. I rushed to the bathroom.

I was confused: why did I have an upset stomach over something I ate all the time and was always comfortable with? I reflected over what I was doing then and as my business grew, I was taking less time to engage with my self-development activities, like go for walks in parks, hydrate more, eat healthier, and even exercise. I took responsibility and got super serious about what I was doing every single day with my habits and focused my day around them. As I decreased my overall stress by staying connected with the earth, my stomach issue went away.

Towards the end of 2018, I met a billionaire who changed my life. Naveen Jain is CEO of a lot of the things around the world, ranging from space companies to healthcare. I interviewed him on my Humans 2.0 Podcast and had a blast with him talking about his company, Viome. He told me that he found an exponential technology the government created, originally used for bio-defense, to identify any chemical compound to find out what's making someone sick. He started a company that licensed that technology along with a head senior at

IBM's artificial intelligence department. Together they created a tool that is going to make chronic illness a choice. Illnesses including autoimmune conditions, heart disease, Alzheimer's, allergies, cancer, asthma, obesity, and type 2 diabetes. After I did the Viome test, most of my autoimmune issues like allergies, asthma, stomach, and even my energy and discharge in the bathroom greatly improved.

What I found out when I did the Viome test is that my body had a hard time processing oats, almonds, and spinach. I already knew about the oats because I rarely eat oatmeal but began to experiment with it for fitness reasons. Every time I ate it, my hands would start shedding skin. The biggest takeaways were the almonds and spinach because I was eating them basically every day, and I didn't know they were harming me. What I learned is that just like any organism or anything on this planet, we must constantly be evolving and changing over time. Our gut microbiome also changes every few months, depending on your activity, food, stress, sleep, antibiotic, or drug use. When I removed the almonds and spinach, my digestion greatly improved, and my stomach stopped hurting.

For lunch I was eating what I thought was a healthy salad, but it turns out spinach was just not compatible with my body at that time. Today, I can eat spinach completely fine because I removed it and slowly began to introduce it cooked in small quantities. But back then, it was giving me stomach issues that made me go to the bathroom uncontrollably, and combined with my lack of taking those mid-afternoon strolls, my body stressed out and in turn impacted my state of mind, mood, and performance.

Social anxiety is usually followed with some sort of an abdominal issue with your stomach. I remember growing up as a kid, I would be in and out of doctor's offices because my stomach was always hurting. Of course, I ate a terrible diet, but looking back, I recall almost always spending extended time in the bathroom before any sort of social event. In fact, there was even a time where I got surgery to take my appendix out. I have no idea why what was inflaming my appendix, but without a doubt, my anxiety, as well as food choices and overall lifestyle, helped create that issue. I discovered that research from the Division of Behavioral Medicine and Clinical Psychology at Cincinnati Children's Hospital Medical Center found a correlation with youths between abdominal issues and pains and overall anxiety in a study.

Decreasing your stress is critical for your mental health and how your body processes and digests what you eat. If you have followed the guidelines in the sections above about the kinds of food you should be eating, you are off to a good start. 80% of the work is done with a standard, non-processed healthy diet. However, if you want to go to the other 20%, then I highly recommend purchasing the Viome test.

You do not **need** to buy a test that can show you on your phone exactly what you should or shouldn't be eating; however, Viome is worthy of the minimal investment.

## Sleep Like a Baby

Here's the thing I realized about sleep. We distract ourselves all the time during the day for good and bad reasons. Walking, talking with friends, eating, watching, playing with your phone, working, etc. One of the rare instances where it's just you and your mind is when you try to go to sleep at night. This is why most people rely on taking some sort of sleep medication, prescribed or not prescribed, like alcohol or smoking weed. There is a real biochemical aspect when it comes to sleep, which is tightly correlated with our overall health, and there is another psychological side that involves much more and has to do with your identity, your purpose, regrets, and much greyer areas of life.

Taking any kind of substance that can noticeably shift your state of mind, like alcohol, sugar, or cannabis, is not good for your long term sleep hygiene. It's not an issue taking these substances every once in a while, but it's particularly alarming being reliant on these chemicals to sleep. I remember in my dark moments I couldn't fall asleep without some form of a substance to forcibly shut off my brain. It was such a problem that I receive emails and messages from my readers. You would be surprised to hear how many people are physically dependent on alcohol for sleep. I receive regular emails from relatively successful professionals who mention that their body does not stop shaking until they get a drink of alcohol to put their mind at ease. If you feel you are addicted to any substance, especially where there is a very real chemical dependence, I advise seeking professional help and potentially going to a rehabilitation program. It is the most loving type of self-care and you won't regret it.

Sleep is defined as being in a waking conscious state, and then in an unconscious state of not being awake, which you can't do with a substance, because going to sleep, while substance induced, you just knock or pass out, but the user doesn't voluntarily fall asleep. Sugar has been notoriously documented over the years as disrupting your sleep due to a blood glucose crash. A study from 2016 found that those who eat a diet low in fiber and high in saturated fat and sugar are associated with lighter, less restorative sleep with more interruptions. Your body constantly needs energy to stay alive and complete it's bodily functions. If you wake up in the middle of the night, that may be because your body ran out of blood glucose and is searching for more energy. Please refer to the section above on food for the importance of your sleep.

## "Sleep is the Golden Chain that Binds Health and our Bodies Together" – Thomas Dekker

## 13 Keys to Sleeping like a Baby

1. **Eliminate processed food** like junk snack foods, sugar, alcohol, etc.
2. **Eat a well-balanced whole foods meal** filled with healthy forms of fat, protein, and carbohydrates to fuel your body's recovery during sleep.
3. **Don't eat or drink anything** right before bed. You want your last meal to be consumed a minimum of 2-3 hours before you sleep, including any fluids like water, to ensure an uninterrupted sleeping pattern without going to the bathroom.
4. **Exercise in the morning or afternoon.** Tire your physical body out via cardio, lifting weights or even just trying to reach 10,000 steps (we will cover physical movement in later subsections)
5. **Participate in a body relaxation t**echnique like stretching deeply or a yoga session you can watch a YouTube video.
6. **Limit your caffeine** intake to 1 cup of coffee before noon or as early as possible. If you must drink caffeine later on in the day, stick to lower caffeine sources like green tea.
7. **Engage in a regular meditation** practice to relieve your mind and decrease anxiety around intrusive thoughts that may cause panic at night.
8. **Anchored Sleep Breathing -** Each time you inhale and exhale, create a vowel sound effect and anchor it to your inhale, and a slightly different sound for your exhale. For example, breathe in play in your head AAAH-HHH, and when you breathe out, play OOOOOO in your head.
9. **Sleep Is Sacred.** Imagine your bedroom as an altar for one of the most important things in life: sleep. You should only sleep in your bed and nothing else except for engaging with a partner. Do not play with your phone or watch TV before falling asleep. Try reading a book to put yourself to sleep. I recommend a book that will not get your head thinking too much.
10. **Magnesium and Tea.** In the section above, we mentioned how important magnesium is for decreasing anxiety, but it also works as a relaxant for sleep. It may also be worthwhile to drink Yogi Soothing Caramel Bedtime tea as well.
11. **Write down your thoughts,** on a piece of paper and capture what you

are grateful for today and what went right and what you look forward to doing tomorrow.
12. **Don't fall asleep watching TV.** Fall asleep reading a book. Our subconscious can be accessed during sleep, which moves our conscious mind during the day. What you do during sleep is surprisingly important and leaving your TV on in the background is not the best environment for sleep.
13. **White Noise or Binaural Beats.** At times it can be useful to put in your wireless headphones and play some white noise or binaural beats, which are sounds created for ambience to focus your brain on the sounds over your thoughts.

## Substances of Our Society (Drugs)

I felt particularly compelled to write this subsection. It is worth noting, aside from some addiction to sugar, I have never experienced a legitimate physical addiction. If you need help, please call your doctor or other professional healthcare practitioner. There's no point in trying to hide shame and think you can beat an addictive compound and potentially getting hurt over just going to see professional help. In this section, I highlight four chemical compounds that are the most used drugs in the world.

It's important to note that according to the National Institute on Alcohol Abuse, nearly 88,005 people (more men than women) die from alcohol-related causes annually, making alcohol the third leading preventable cause of death in the United States. The first is tobacco, and the second is poor diet and physical inactivity.

### *Sugar*

I can write an entire book on this topic alone. Sugar is the biggest gateway drug in our society that continues to keep people anxious, tired, lazy, and not themselves. Growing up, I routinely remember before or after school, I would stop by the store and buy bags of candy or stop at a drive-thru and buy donuts and eat them. What happens? After eating them and providing my body energy with the sugar, it is quickly used up by your brain and creates the exact environment needed for anxiety to flourish and thrive.

**Issue**: Sugar has been shown to be more physically addictive than cocaine. A study from *Frontiers in Psychiatry* explored that sugar is often used to make foods more appealing. This could lead to habituation and even in some cases, addiction, contributing to the obesity epidemic and, in my opinion, the mental health epidemic as well. The study goes on to mention – "a review of the evolutionary aspects of feeding and how they have shaped the human brain to function in 'survival mode' signaling to 'eat as much as you can while you can.' This leads to our present understanding of how the dopaminergic system is involved in reward and its functions in hedonistic rewards, like eating highly palatable foods, and drug addiction."

**Solution**: try naturally low glycemic sugars like stevia, erythritol, monk fruit, etc.

Quitting cold turkey may not even be an option for some of you. When I tried to quit sugar, my body couldn't handle it; I folded and ate more sugar. My favorite sugary desserts are ice cream and brownies by far. I could eat an entire tub of chocolate chip cookie dough or a red velvet pint with brownies with absolutely no hesitation.

What I began to do is seek a closer alternative. I would go to the supermarket and buy frozen fruit like berries and either eat them straight up or blend them together with some coconut milk and make nice cream. If you haven't heard of this, it's a way to make a frozen dessert with the same texture of ice cream by blending frozen fruits together. I did this for two weeks and slowly began to wean the amount I was eating and eventually transitioned to eating no sugar.

Sugar is in almost every single processed food. Avoid processed foods, avoid sugar, stick to natural sources of sugar, but rely on fats and fiber as a fuel source. If you spend your entire day focusing on not eating sugar, you will eventually fold and eat sugar. The key is to focus on being properly fed and hydrated with healthy forms of food so that you eventually are not as tempted to devour a tasty, devilish treat.

### *Caffeine*

First and foremost, coffee is not bad for you, usually. I'm not that bad of a guy to tell you to quit coffee. But if you're reading this book and on your 4th coffee, there might be a problem. Reality is caffeine is a drug that has fueled the productivity of most of human history. USE IT with intention. I drink a single cup of coffee every morning. On a long day, a bit past noon, I'll drink some green tea. If you don't drink coffee because you are aware of the possible anxiety effects it can have, I recommend green tea. Why? There's some caffeine, but also a chemical called L-Theanine. which has been shown to regulate and calm the nervous system. It's nature's perfect balance between caffeine and a chemical that can help you more efficiently process it and actually calm you down.

I hate to break it to you, but that large coffee you've ordered for the second time today is not just loaded with an insane amount of caffeine but also sugar and chemicals. It is not actually giving you long-lasting energy. I still drink coffee, but have learned that I personally have a super-fast caffeine metabolism, which means when I drink coffee, my brain quickly absorbs it, and you know what happens? Thoughts start rushing and I might get anxious and jittery, even if I have nothing to be anxious about.

I've learned I need to combine my coffee with some sort of a fat source to slow the absorption down in my nervous system or drink it very slowly. I drink Bulletproof coffee on occasion, which is coffee, grass-fed butter, and MCT oil. Bulletproof coffee is widely used around the world by high performers who are looking for more sustained energy without the crash. Like everything, it's not for everybody but give it a shot.

Dear Adolescents,
A study from 2016 by the Department of Psychology and Neuroscience and Center for Neuroscience at the University of Colorado found that adolescents who consume caffeine have a higher correlation of increased anxiety-related behavior in adulthood. Adolescent caffeine consumption decreases adrenal gland sensitivity in adulthood. Most alarmingly, adolescent caffeine consumption increases activity in the central nucleus of the amygdala in adulthood. The amygdala is largely responsible for our fear based emotions, survival instincts, and memory.

Again, I'm not saying that having a cup of coffee is bad. In fact, it can be one of life's great pleasures if used properly. But, like everything, don't abuse the tool, don't let the tool control the user, and take responsibility for knowing it is not a harmless substance.

*Alcohol*
Most people today drink alcohol not for the occasional celebration, but to medicate themselves. Unfortunately, I commonly hear from the subscribers who listen to my podcast that they suffer with extreme social anxiety and some of them cope with it with alcohol. I remember I received an email from a lady who told me she literally can't shut down her nervous system and go to sleep without drinking alcohol.

I don't think there's anything terrible about having the occasional drink, but drinking frequently sets your nervous system up for physical dependence and teaches your mind to only be calm with an external substance like alcohol. The real danger with alcohol is that it's everywhere, just like sugar. Again, I don't think there's anything wrong with enjoying a drink with some buddies. But there

IS something wrong with after your work shift, you routinely hit up the bar and drink to shut your brain off, so you don't have to think about your life.

If you have been drinking every single day and have tried quitting before, I highly recommend going to AA to get some help. Alcohol is a serious drug and there are people who have been there done that and can help you slowly wean off and not be dependent. The Anxiety and Depression Association of America (ADAA) notes that 20 percent of people dealing with social anxiety disorder suffer from some form of alcohol abuse or dependence. In fact, a twin study done by the Depression and Anxiety Association of America found some pretty phenomenal results. Social anxiety disorder had the strongest association with alcohol use disorder out of all of the other anxiety disorders. They even found that if you want to tackle alcoholism, you might want to tackle handling your social anxiety first.

Alcohol is the biggest social lubricant of our society today. You go to an event, party, wedding, family gathering where there might be some hesitancy or awkwardness when it comes to social interactions, so, you grab a drink from the bar. I'm not going to be that guy that tells you to not drink alcohol, but be mindful of how you react to people under the influence and when sober. I'll be the first one to tell you, I became conscious that I had social anxiety the first time I got drunk at a college party because all of a sudden, my brain let me talk to people.

Find healthier coping mechanisms to deal with the stress of social interactions because alcohol is a terrible medicine for prolonged use. Alcohol use is correlated with many other negative mental health issues, ages you faster, and is not good for your soul. Again, if you need help please seek professional guidance because alcohol is not a harmless joke. The National Institute on Alcohol Abuse reports that an estimated 88,000 people die from alcohol-related causes annually, making alcohol the third leading preventable cause of death in the United States.

## *Cannabis*

Depending on who you hang out with or what you see or read, you might think smoking weed is the worst thing for your anxiety or the best thing ever to calm down. It's clear that cannabis isn't as dangerous to justify the reefer madness craze of the 1900's but it's also not like drinking water without any issues or side effects. Just like alcohol, I believe there is also the right place, right time for one of the most commonly used drugs in the world, cannabis.

However, for those prone to anxiety, it is very common for cannabis to possibly trigger anxiety for you and spiral thoughts out of control. The impact of cannabis on an individual is so widely varied there isn't clear 100% science on this substance, but there is some. But, one thing is clear, smoking ANYTHING is not good for you. Whether you smoke weed or you grab some grass from your garden, it's still terrible for your lungs and breathing. Our lungs were created to utilize only one compound: air.

I wasn't going to include this section in the book, but I live in Boston, Massachusetts, where cannabis has recently become recreationally legal. However, there seems to be a false assumption floating around that because it's legal, it must be completely 100% harmless for you. The reality is that weed, marijuana, cannabis sativa - whatever you want to call it - is still a drug. If you are experiencing social anxiety and you are a frequent consumer, consider lowering the frequency of use or eliminating it completely. Nobody has the same biochemistry, and it is impossible to learn how it impacts you in the short and long term.

In June of 2017, the University of Washington did a study on the effects of marijuana on mental health, and here's what they found:

- Many people report using marijuana to cope with anxiety, **especially those with social anxiety disorder.**
- THC appears to decrease anxiety at lower doses and increase anxiety at higher doses. (Psychoactive component in the plant that gets you "high")
- CBD appears to decrease anxiety at all doses that have been tested. (Non-psychoactive component that does not make you high and is correlated with many potential health benefits).
- There are individual differences in responses to marijuana that are affected by a variety of factors, though tolerance develops over a short period of time with regular use.
- Using marijuana to cope with anxiety may offer some short-term benefit, but well-controlled studies indicate that use of marijuana is associated with increased likelihood of substance use disorders.
- Marijuana use may alleviate some social anxiety disorder related impairments in the short-term but also present **increased risk of harm in the long term especially** in terms of likelihood of alcohol and other substance use disorders.

**Note**: I'm a big proponent of it's not so much about the substance or the tool, but the user at play. That doesn't mean go try crack or heroin; but, we live in a society where major drugs, whether it be substances of mind numbing content like pornography or content online that tells says you are not enough, is accessible at a tap of your finger. Take responsibility for your life and do not be at the whim of massive corporations and influences telling you what to do with your body.

If you feel you are addicted to any of these compounds, especially alcohol, please contact your local AA or NA organizations for help. You are better off checking yourself into a rehabilitation center and doing the work versus hoping this problem leaves you.

## Anxiety Says Move

This book is not for those of you who are trying to get super ripped and lean or even lose a few pounds (although these things might happen as a byproduct). I've said it before, but I don't really care that much about physical health other than the scientific fact that it's tightly correlated to mental health. If you recall at the beginning of this book, I talked a bit about my story and my worst moments walking the streets of Boston at night alone. Looking back, what I was actually doing was one of the few coping mechanisms I sort of learned in life. Walking. Wow, sounds crazy right?

Today we live in a society where you don't have to walk, other than walking from your place to your car, and from your car to your office, and from your office back to your car and then back home. You can get all food, including groceries, delivered to you within an hour and just walk downstairs to let the delivery person inside. Modern conveniences are great, but unfortunately it's not how our evolutionary biology evolved to thrive and be happy.

We were built to move all throughout the day, whether it was finding a fresh source of water, hunting, gathering, or other kinds of physical labor. The irony of this is in today's world we have built hamster wheels called gyms. There is nothing wrong with gyms; I go to the gym almost every single day. The gym is a great battleground and what most people think of when I say get active. However, our bodies were not created to move for one hour heavily and then sit down slouched at our desks for the remainder of the day.

Anxiety is physical. Shallow breaths, heat flashes on your forehead and cheeks, no energy in your body, yet too much energy in your mind. Therefore, doing something physical might indeed ease anxiety. Everyone reading this book has a different starting point. You might have been an athlete your whole life and took physical exercise for granted. Or, you could be just like I used to exist, mostly sedentary my whole life.

If you've never exercised in your life, maybe it's a good idea to start walking.

Ideally, walk outside or head to a gym and walk on a treadmill. Heck, you can even start walking around your house or in your house, even if you live in a small apartment. If you have never exercised before, it's easy to discount this and say, "I'm not an athletic person" or "that's not for me." The reality is, if you have legs, this is for you. If you can't even walk in any capacity, use light weights and do some bicep curls; do whatever you can do to move your body.

**Mini-workouts** are crucial to managing anxiety. If I am going to speak at an event or go somewhere and talk to many people, I will 100% make sure I visit the gym beforehand. I will focus on stretching my muscles, lifting for a short bit, and then go for a run either outside or on the treadmill. Running for a period of time has been scientifically proven to produce what we call an endorphin high. Endorphins work on the same receptors as heroin or morphine you get at the hospital.

Why is this important? Because this is one of the main mechanisms our body uses to manage pain. What's painful for someone with social anxiety? Talking to other people. Using heavy cardio as a temporary bridge for you to get into the experience of what it feels like to talk to people is unbelievably powerful. Again, this is an example of choosing a healthy coping mechanism over a not so healthy method to manage social anxiety.

Aside from cardio, moving throughout the day is so important for managing most kinds of anxiety. I will go on a walk in the middle of the day, a bit past noon. I try my best to aim for 30-60 minutes while listening to an audiobook/podcast/ or sometimes nothing. But anything can help, including just a 10 minute walk. As you get into the habit of taking daily walks, aside from the morning at the gym, you will fairly quickly notice your anxiety decrease, and a more manageable form of your energy rise instead.

The Anxiety and Depression Association of America researchers have found that regular participation in cardio exercise has been shown to decrease tension, increase mood, improve sleep, and improve self-esteem, all factors that can greatly help you manage social anxiety. Another study done at the Rex Sports Medicine Institute, in North Carolina, found that a regular regimen of both cardio and strength training exercises can greatly improve anxiety, similar to those of meditation and regular relaxation.

If you are a workaholic *cough* I mean entrepreneur like me, and addicted to getting things done, you can also barter with your anxiety. At times, I will schedule meetings where I don't need to be looking at a computer all in a row for a duration of 2-3 hours and go on a massive walk. 9 times out of 10, because anxiety is being decreased and I got blood flow moving to my brain, my conversations will go much better, and I feel like I am on target with my thoughts and mood.

Overall, just moving your body is a fundamental aspect of life that many of us are detached from, and this leads to consequences for both our physical health and our mental health. Have a strength training regimen throughout the week, mixed in with a healthy dose of cardio, and throughout your hour to hour day, put in some mini exercises you can do anywhere, from your office to the cafeteria.

**Exercise:** Look at your schedule and find 4 slots of 5-10 minutes where you can get up from your seat and do some exercises. You could do squats in the bathroom, go for a brisk walk, perform 10 push-ups, do jumping jacks, or run in place for 60 seconds. Schedule these mini exercise breaks in your calendar if you are unsure you will remember throughout the day.

## Body <—> Mind Feedback Loop

The mind and body have a very interesting relationship with each other. Often times what will happen is in times of either anxiety or confidence, the mind will look at the body, and at times the body will look at the mind for confirmation. If you have heard of this notion before, you may think it is not based off science and just a theory. Well, a study from the School of Social Work at Georgia State University found that talk-therapy interventions in altering immune system parameters and enhancing the body's ability to combat disease as well as the impact of chronic stress of poverty on immune system function is very much real.

**Example**: you are binging Netflix shows and you look at the clock and it's 2 am. You've been laying down on the couch in the exact same spot for the past 5 hours. You might get a thought that creates uncertainty, like, "Why am I doing this?" or " I wonder what other people my age are doing right now?" or "Should I get up and go to sleep...nah, I'm not gonna be able to fall asleep." Your anxious but lethargic body then looks at your mind, and anxious thoughts begins to rise and cause your body to tense up. Your mind and body will hype each other up. In both good ways and bad ways, but especially with anxious feelings and thoughts, your body and mind really need to be in sync.

**Example 2:** You're hungry. You go down to your typical American fast food joint and grab a burger, fries, and soda. You eat it. Your mind gives you the feeling that you're full. But, your body realizes everything you just ate is full of crap and has no nutrients to utilize for necessary biological functions. Now, your body is anxious and slowly begins to send the message to your mind. Your mind says no wait, we just ate. What are you talking about? This creates a conscious or unconscious panic state, which then proceeds to create more inflammation in your brain on top of the junk food you just ate.

Behavioral studies like one done from the Department of Psychiatry at the Ohio State Institute for Behavioral Medicine Research has demonstrated that stressful events, depression, and unhealthy meals work together to enhance inflammation. This is quite alarming considering inflammation is the common link among the leading causes of death around the world. The key to mental health then is not necessarily all about the brain and the mind, but also how the body comes in and interacts with our state of mind.

## Take care of your body, as if it is the outward skin of the unconscious mind.

## Take care of your mind, as if it is the inward engine of your operational soul.

**Exercise:** Sit down with this newly formed realization about how the body and mind work and write down any instances where you have experienced a mind body connection or even disconnection. Example - when I walk around, my anxiety drops and I'm able to harness my anxious energy into better thoughts and ideas.

# 5.

# Learning How to Be Human

A critical element I had to learn about social anxiety is that we are very rarely taught how to authentically communicate ourselves to the world. The education system teaches you geography and how photosynthesis works, but they don't teach you how a human works, including but not limited to how to deal with your own emotions, how to express yourself with others, and how to build social skills. If you haven't learned something before and didn't necessarily have the most intuitive and teaching parents, you could potentially develop social anxiety. Learning how to be a human is a critical intervention in any person who has issues communicating themselves to the world, although it's definitely not a magic bullet as many people who have social anxiety have great social skills.

If you don't have social skills, it's just because you weren't taught. How can you judge yourself for something you have never learned before? Even though you have a problem, you shouldn't feel judgment or feel ashamed. Not because there's something wrong with you, but because you simply have not learned how to communicate with other people. On my journey, a critical piece that I had to learn is the actual science of human behavior. The science of how to talk to people and how you convey yourself to others and how they perceive you when you are talking with an individual or group and expressing an idea.

I remember sitting on my living room couch and watching all of the YouTube videos I could possibly find, taking notes, and testing out theories of communication. As always, some of the experiments I ran worked for me, while others did not work or were not the most efficient use of my time.

I vividly remember sitting down on my living room couch with my iPad and binge watching videos from Vanessa Van Edwards, a behavioral investigator at a human behavior research lab, the Science of People. I was taking frantic notes because I couldn't believe that there was a way to learn how to be less awkward and how to just express what I didn't know how to say to others. It wasn't so much the words and what to say that I found interesting, but rather how people potentially perceive who you are in a conversation based off what you DON'T say and other elements outside of verbal communication. My findings and research led me down a rabbit hole of human behavior, and I began studying this as if I was looking up how an animal lives and functions. We often think we are unconsciously competent at human natural givens like eating, moving, talking, and communicating with others, but it's just not that simple.

## Layers of Social Anxiety

When I began tackling shyness and social anxiety, I didn't do too much research other than how do I learn the right body language to present myself to the world. But, I wish I did my research from people who have done the scientific work to understand the backend of what's actually going on when someone is having trouble being themselves in the world. I had the utmost pleasure of interviewing Ellen Hendriksen, a clinical psychologist who serves on the faculty at Boston University's Center for Anxiety and Related Disorders and is the author of another amazing and very useful book - *How to Be Yourself: Quiet Your Inner Critic and Rise Above Social Anxiety,* which I highly recommend.

When I interviewed Ellen on my Humans 2.0 Podcast Episode 99, she made some profoundly scientific observations relating to what I thought being shy meant. Ellen went on to tell me that "Social anxiety is a perception that there is something wrong or deficient about us, and unless we work hard to hide that perceived deficiency, we'll be revealed or judged or rejected." Wow. I've never heard a more accurate statement in my entire life. What Ellen said next went on to change my life and moved my abstract ideas and implementation into concrete objective layers to reverse my social anxiety.

Ellen says that our perceived deficiencies tend to fall into four categories.

1. **Physical appearance.** We might be worried that people will notice that

we're fat, that our face looks weird, or we're wearing the same clothes from yesterday and get rejected.
2. **Signs of Anxiety Itself.** Are your hands shaking? Can you properly pronounce words or are you too nervous or are you blushing? Maybe everyone can now see your armpit sweat stains and judge or mock you.
3. **Social Skills.** Do you worry that you have no social skills? You don't know what to talk about with people because you think you're stupid or not funny. So, you ramble on and on nervously or you don't say anything at all.
4. **Entire Personality or Character.** We might be nervous because we have deep conscious or unconscious doubts and insecurities about who we are as a person.

Ellen went on to tell me that the last 2 categories of social skills and entire personality are the most common deficiencies that lead to social anxiety. In the chapters following, we will go over exactly how to systematically rid yourself of each deficiency depending on your category.

## Words are Sort of Meaningless

Did you know that most of our communication with others has nothing to do with words? The number is anywhere between 7-55% of our communication has to do with the actual words and language we use to convey a message. The rest is a mixture of your vocal tone, body language, facial mannerisms, and other seemingly hidden and subtle changes that have existed for thousands of years. Humans use these to authentically pick up on each other's truth amidst the puzzle of language and interconnectedness. What a lot of people don't realize is that if you are not a naturally charismatic person, and you did not have super social parents that have taught you the ins and outs of communication, then you are more than likely going to be a socially awkward person by nature.

It's okay to be shy at times and everyone might experience it to a degree. However, being shy at times like going to a crowded party is different than living in social anxiety, a bubble of your own creation of being afraid to talk to people because you just don't know how. Who knew that making direct eye contact with others was important to establishing a connection built on trust? Who knew that depending how you stand and what you do with your leg position enables the other person to unconsciously realize you are socially anxious and uncomfortable? All of these things that I learned then, and then looking back at my life, were making perfect sense. It's not like people didn't like me, but they thought I didn't like them based on my body language and other mannerisms that presented to people that I was shy and anxious.

I began to learn more about body language: what is a person's face telling me about what they are actually feeling? what does my body do when I am uncomfortable? Am I my twirling my legs around and my biting my nails? do I have a concerned look on my face or are my shoulders hunched backwards to give the feeling that I'm crouched down? All of these are massive elements to learning about social anxiety because if you are acting a certain way in your body, your body is going to send a message to your mind and your mind is going to look at your body and get even more anxious and freaked out.

Perhaps the most important element to body language is not necessarily how it will make you feel but how it will make other people feel. For the longest time, I genuinely thought people didn't like me and whenever I would speak, people didn't like what they heard. It's not even because my words weren't powerful or legitimate, but I just didn't know how to properly communicate words, let alone other aspects of communication that can be more powerful than words like body language and other visual and vocal cues.

**Focus on How to Improve Your Communication Skills:**

1. Body and Neck Posture. Pretend there's a string that pulls up your head straight at all times. Stand with your shoulders back straight like a Superman pose.
2. Use your hands and open palms when you speak with others naturally. Don't get overactive and pretend as if you're directing puppets and don't keep your hands by your side, not moving or unseen to the person speaking with you.
3. Don't frantically tap your legs or twist them together. You want to have a stable foundation from your feet as to where you are standing with someone else.
4. Exercising to release energy, as well as body relaxation techniques like Yoga and stretching, can greatly benefit someone's body stability on a daily basis.
5. Unclench your jaw by leaving a tiny amount of space in between your lips. Be mindful of your facial expressions at all times. Are you smiling? Are you frowning? Do you look annoyed? How would you look to a bystander?
6. Don't breathe like a submachine gun. Focus on taking somewhat deep slow controlled breaths through your nose to the bottom of your lungs, in and out.

7. Practice talking with clear articulation. Read a book and try to pronounce every single word clearly again and again. You can do this in front of the mirror and other exercises with your lips to improve voice clarity; don't mumble.
8. Unless you don't have social anxiety, always speak louder than you think you sound. Having a loud and clear voice will make you a beacon of communication, not an invisible shy person.
9. Experiment. There is not one magic formula that fits all. Play around and don't get too serious. You can always practice with strangers because you'll never see them again.

## Pretend You're an Extrovert Sometimes

I stumbled across a lecture video from the one and only social psychologist and professor in Toronto, Jordan Peterson. He was talking about social anxiety, human behavior, going to parties, and how to begin to tackle that ambiguous monster. He said most people that go to a party and have social anxiety don't look at the main crowd of people because they are afraid. Well, what if you did look at the crowd of people or whoever you thought was intimidating you socially? What if you make some direct eye contact? Peterson goes on to mention that a major part of your fear is actually because you are trying to avoid looking and gaining information. Why? Because you are too busy mentally projecting in your head how terrible this social scenario is and you don't want to look at that. You are facing the unknown on the outside, and potentially false known's in your head. Not looking at people, and therefore not knowing how they feel, or think, is ramping up your anxiety even more. I used to do this at all kinds of social gatherings I went to before - unknowingly. It's almost as if when you have social anxiety, you are treating your social fears like Medusa; you can't make direct eye contact or else you're screwed, which is in fact the opposite to tackling social anxiety.

Do you remember our definition of an introvert? Introversion is defined as the tendency to be concerned with one's own thoughts and feelings rather than with external things. As introverts, we are usually focused on the inside world, which is great and has many benefits, like the ability to take your dreams and bring them into reality. This is why many successful people who have done amazing things at a global or historic level have been introverts. So, first understand the tremendous power of introversion. However, sometimes we can be a little bit too introverted. Sometimes, depending on our life's path, somewhere on the road of introversion, we took a sharp right into social anxiety and shyness because something unexpected happened to us. Being introverted is a good thing; shy and socially anxious, not so much.

But, just like everything in life, you don't always want to act in a singular way. Life is full of scenarios that may require you to adjust yourself for optimal results. Sometimes it's good to not be an introvert. How? If an introvert is someone who is primarily focused on the internal world, it might be wise to run an experiment to begin to focus more on the outside world, like an extrovert. Let me ask you some questions. On your drive to or from work that you take almost every single day,

Do you remember the environment?
Do you remember what color the trees were?
Do you remember which stores were open or closed?
Do you remember the people using the crosswalk to get across the street?

You probably don't. Your brain was running on auto-pilot, super focused on the internal world. Your thoughts, emotions, moods, insecurities, fears were all boiling and processing in the background of your life. Thinking and processing information is unbelievably important to sound mental health; however, participating in what most introvert's do (negative self-talk) too much in their head, can create social anxiety and living in your fears much worse. I challenge you to genuinely look at your environment, where you are, what it looks like, and don't take what you see for granted. I believe the worst mindset someone can be in is thinking they know everything about life. Thinking that they've seen everything, been there, done that syndrome, like most young adults and teenagers, is a disease. Try to see the world again through a child-like wonder state of awe and focus as much as you can on the outside external world.

Now, what separates those who read a book and just massage themselves mentally and the people who actually get up and implement what they learned into their daily lives and transform the fidelity of their experience of the world? One word: FLOW.

## The Ultimate Learning Highway (FLOW)

What's FLOW? "Flow" is the term used by researchers for optimal states of consciousness; those peak moments of total absorption where the self disappears, time flies, and all aspects of performance goes through the roof. It's those moments where you are doing something that engages you in the moment so much, 2 hours later you look at the clock and you're like, "Wait, what just happened? That felt like 15 minutes?"

If you have ever heard of FLOW you have probably heard it associated alongside a gentlemen by the name of Steven Kotler, eight time *New York Times* Bestselling author. I've had the honor of speaking with Steven twice on my Humans 2.0 Podcast to talk about a variety of topics from neuroscience to the future of how we're going to do everything. Steven told me a crazy story of how he even got down this path of exploring FLOW, utilizing it in his daily life, and teaching it to thousands of others at the Flow Genome Project. Steven came down with a very serious form of Lyme disease that left him immobile and sick in bed for three years. Steven's sickness came to the point where it got into his brain and short-term and long-term memory were gone. He could barely focus, barely function, and was only able to work a couple of hours a day at best; he even contemplated suicide.

Eventually, a friend of Steven's came to this apartment and refused to leave until he got up and went with her to the beach to go surfing. It was a rocky start at first, but eventually Steven got up on the board and had a crazy vivid experience. He kept on going back and surfing again and again for the next 6-8 months. Steven went from 10% functional to 20% functional to about 80% functional. Not only was Steven feeling way better, but he went on a giant quest to figure out what the hell was going on.

He discovered that these states of consciousness have names called flow states. He also learned very soon after that they have a profound impact on the immune system and nervous system, which explained why he was feeling much better. It didn't take Steven long to figure out that the same state of consciousness that was helping him go from seriously subpar back to normal was helping normal people go all the way up to Superman around the world.

In a 2008 study, Johns Hopkins neuroscientist Charles Limb used functional magnetic resonance imaging (fMRI) to examine the brains of improv jazz musicians in flow - musicians that were in the middle of their moment, flowing with music and feeling a timeless integration with themselves, instrument and the 4 dimensional reality created with music. Charles found the dorsolateral prefrontal cortex, an area of the brain best known for self-monitoring, literally deactivated. For context, self-monitoring is the voice of doubt or inner critic.

Since flow is a fluid state—where problem solving is nearly automatic—second guessing only slows down that process. When the dorsolateral prefrontal cortex goes quiet, those guesses are cut off at the source, leaving barely any self-monitoring. The result is liberation. We act without hesitation. Creativity becomes more free-flowing, risk taking becomes less frightening, and the combination lets us flow at a far faster rate. It's almost as if that movie *Limitless,* about taking a drug to access all 100% of your brain, is the exact opposite; we are better when less of our brain is being used.

So, why am I mentioning all of this about FLOW? Learning how to put yourself in the FLOW state of mind is the highway out of social anxiety. Reality is, if you want to learn and implement anything in this book, it's not about being a reader. It's about becoming a critical thinker and implementer in your own life. There's so much to learn that unless you have a photographic memory, you MUST learn how to FLOW to be able to get past your mind's inner critic that tells you, "This is stupid," when you sit down and meditate. You don't even have a fighting chance against your neuroticism and introversion unless you are using FLOW to momentarily bypass your brain's inner critic and create a new experience that causes your brain to say "Woah, we could do that?"

Here's how to get into FLOW. The following 18 FLOW state triggers come from research undertaken by the Flow Genome Project led by Steven Kotler and Jamie Wheal.

**There are 4 groups of FLOW Trigger:**

1. **Psychological**
2. **Environmental**
3. **Social**
4. **Creative**

*Psychological Triggers*

1. **Intensely Focused Attention** – One of the primary purposes of flow state is to help you focus on a particular task; however, to hack into the flow state in the first place, you must be in a position that allows you to strongly focus your attention on your goals. This also means multi-tasking is out. Flow demands singular and solitude action.
2. **Clear Goals** – When you have clear goals, your mind doesn't have to wonder what to do next. You know what you're doing and why you're doing it. Also, don't focus on the finish line; focus on running the race, the NOW, the present moment. Many are getting distracted by their past, future, or self. Focus on the clarity of your goals. It gives you certainty.
3. **Immediate Feedback** – This trigger is a partner with clear goals. Clear goals tell us what we're doing; immediate feedback tells us how to do it

better. If we know how to improve performance in real time, the mind doesn't go off in search of clues for betterment.
4. **The Challenge/Skill Ratio** – You may have heard about the concept of a stress curve where there is a scale of low stress and low performance. At the other end, is the high stress and low performance, but in the middle of the scale is the optimal level of stress correlating to peak performance. The Flow Challenge/Skill ratio exists near (but not on) the midline between boredom and anxiety. We need a progressive balance between boredom and anxiety or tension and relaxation. If you can keep yourself in that sweet spot, then you can drive attention into the present and maximize the amount of flow in your daily living.

## *Environmental Triggers*

1. **High Consequences** – If your neck is on the line, then you are driven into the zone. An athlete, big wave surfer, for example, may need to drop into a 50-foot wave to pull this trigger. But the shy guys may only need to cross the room and speak to an attractive woman to pull this trigger. This doesn't always mean physical danger; this can also be an emotional, mental, and social risk. You must be willing to take risks. It's that sense of adventure and potential for failure that will drive you.
2. **Rich Environment** – This means an environment with lots of novelty, unpredictability, and complexity. Novelty means surrounding yourself with a rich environment that involves finding things that will catch and keep your attention. Unpredictability means being able to step outside your comfort zone and face the unknown. Complexity means increasing the depth and breadth of your knowledge by seeking out information from many different sources or viewpoints.
3. **Deep Embodiment** – This means total physical awareness. When you can harness the power of your whole body, paying attention to the task at hand, you will feel unstoppable. This also means paying attention to multiple sensory streams at once. Not only our five senses but also our proprioception and vestibular awareness.

## *Social Triggers*

1. **Serious Concentration** – In extreme sports, for example, concentration

is highly required to avoid injury or death. You need to be aware of your teammates and opponents. If they lose focus and start thinking about what's for dinner, or other things, they'll quickly be overrun. It can also help to ensure that everyone has their maximum attention to the here and now, blocking off other distractions.

2. **Shared, Clear Goals** – Groups need to be clear about what their collective goal is in order for the flow state to be achieved. Group flow is a progressive balancing act. Creating a goal that provides enough focus so each team member can tell when they are close to a solution, but one that is open enough for creativity to exist.

3. **Good Communication** – A group flow needs constant communication. The conversation must flow forward. Listen closely to what is being said, accept it, and build upon it. Nothing blocks flow more than ignoring or negating a group member.

4. **Familiarity** – A sports team may be composed of a group with different languages, cultures, and beliefs, but everyone needs to be familiar with each other. Everyone needs to share a common language, a shared knowledge base, and communication style based on unspoken understandings. There must be unity, in thoughts and in action. Everyone must be on the same page, and, when novel insights arise, momentum is not lost due to the need for a lengthy explanation.

5. **Equal Participation and Skill Level** – When you have a team with an equal role in the project, flow is most likely to happen in your group. Teamwork is the key, and everyone must be involved. All members should have similar skill levels.

6. **Risk** – It applies to groups in the same way that it applies to individuals. When there is an element of risk, people are more motivated to work hard and make things happen. Without challenges, the tasks may appear boring. There's also no creativity without failure, and there's no group flow without the risk of failure. **This risk can't be just physical; it also applies to mental, creative, etc.**

7. **Sense of Control** – It's important to combine autonomy (being free to do what you want) with competence (being good at what you do) in group flow. Whatever the situation you are in, getting to choose your own challenges and having the necessary skills to surmount them is beneficial.

8. **Close Listening** – When you are listening closely to the present conversation, your responses will flow, and conversation will progress naturally. Innovation shouldn't be blocked in a group flow. But if one or more team

members are talking simultaneously, you keep yourselves away from listening to what is really said and working from there.
9. **Always Say Yes** – Now, don't mistake this for always saying yes to everything. This means that interactions should be additive more than argumentative. This element is about being open to trying new things, even if they sound like a bad idea. All input into the group should be additive, not negative. The goal is the momentum, togetherness, and innovation that comes from intensifying each other's ideas and actions.

*Creativity Triggers*

"Creativity triggers flow, then flow enhances creativity."

If you look under the hood of creativity, here is what you see:

1. **Pattern Recognition** – The brain's ability to break down existing patterns, colors, data, shapes, movements, sounds, concepts, successes, risks, failures, etc., and create new ideas using those patterns by linking new ideas, and engaging in risk-taking.
2. **Risk-Taking** – The courage to bring those new ideas into the world. Will the new concept be well-received, or will it be panned? All creativity requires an element of risk and courage.

**Personally, the following are what put me in a state of flow:**

- Mindfulness or Transcendental Meditation
- Writing, including my thoughts as they enter into my stream of consciousness
- Walking, running or intensive forms of exercise
- Deep conversation 1 on 1 or in an intimate group
- Speaking on stage in front of hundreds or thousands
- Cooking
- Music - getting into the rhythm of a beat or song

Schedule your day around FLOW to encourage the least resistance learning vs the resistance of your old previous habits. Get smart and learn how you react depending on each part of the day. Are you more focused in the morning? Are you a night owl? Can you only focus when you're listening to a certain kind of music? The combination of learning how to enter into a state of FLOW alongside the pursuit of becoming a less socially anxious person is a powerful weapon that can fly you faster than a rocket.

**Exercise:** Study yourself, determine how you get into FLOW, and fit it into your day as much as possible. Schedule periods of the day where you are synchronizing FLOW with the deep work you do on yourself or any tasks that need to be done.

**Example** - I wake up, meditate, journal, go for a walk, and have a cup of coffee. This almost always gets me into a state of FLOW, which then I harness to write or finish any very important tasks I need to take care of for 1 to 3 hours at a time.

## Changing the Way you Think About Yourself

If you've already focused on all the chapters we've mentioned previously about eating healthy and living in the truth, and began taking steps of applying them into your own life, you are already on the way to changing how you think about yourself when you are by yourself. However, you will need to undergo a consistent amount of change required on a daily basis to undo the wrongdoings of yesterday. Not in a negative way, like rationalizing that because you overate 2000 calories, you are punishing yourself by going to the gym. Instead, just realizing how the human mind works with habits and how much easier it is to just slip in and do the same thing you have always done; not because you want to, but because it's easier.

I always choose to think in the long term, which can be terrible if you are someone who lacks patience. Personally, I think about myself in 10 year increments. The way I think about it is if I'm 22 right now, I had a conscious transformation at 18, and I've only lived 4 years of my life walking the true path. I personally think it's only fair to gently judge yourself on a journey when I'm double my age at 44. There's a lot of gunk you've gotta clear out that you've been unconsciously building in your psychology for decades. This is not going to come easy.

There is no linear path of growth where tomorrow you're better, the day after you are even better, and the day after that you are better than the day before. I wish life's growth was linear, but that's just not the case. You need a healthy dose of self-love and self-forgiveness to be able to forgive your past self for the things that you did in survival mode and truly love yourself. This section will help push you towards recreating the identity of the person you are deep down internally and want to outwardly extrude to the outside world.

I interviewed Alex Banayan, author of *The Third Door,* and he let me in on a mind-blowing technique to start changing the way you think about yourself. Identify a few traits that you really like about yourself, traits that are deep and meaningful to you and not shallow on the surface. Traits like honesty or being warm hearted and giving are good examples. Next, focus on each trait one at a time and try to remember what events happened in your life that prove that trait to be true. What you will realize is as you begin doing this activity, your memory will expand on past memories and find new paths of evidence.

We often view our memory as this perfect system that connects what happened in the past to right now and what will happen as a file cabinet of memories we can access at any time. This is very much not the reality of our memories and actually acts like a vast interconnected web of sometimes visible and invisible layers until triggered. Doing this activity will give your brain evidence of what it needs to actually believe in the person you really are deep down, but want to be more like in everyday life.

Do this daily, for as long as you want or need. When Alex told me about this, I immediately dove headfirst and went off a hunch I had about one of my main traits: abiding in the truth. At first when I sat down with a piece of paper, my mind gave me a couple of pretty simple and shallow reasons or past experiences as to why I was truthful that had happened in the past two weeks. As I sat down with myself for an extended period, all of a sudden a handful of memories popped up into my head of my past. These were memories and experiences of myself as a little kid, from the youngest age, demonstrating truth and honesty to myself and others around me.

Another trait I developed was the belief that I was good for humanity and am a proponent of peace and unity, not violence and division. While this might seem quite elementary, I realized that unless we have consciously defined these things on our own, even if we think that's who we are or operate, we may be wrong. What I realized is if you don't define yourself, society and the people around you will do the defining and labeling for you, which has repercussions you don't want.

I don't know about you, but growing up with anxiety, and at times depression, really caused me to suppress so many memories about myself and the events that unfolded. To give myself the opportunity to relax and grow, every couple of months or so, while simply doing random things, I will remember something about my past self that I didn't know in my conscious mind. This is why in the first few chapters you did an exercise that made you sit down and think about the truth of your life. Just giving yourself that private space can do wonders for your mind, as long as it isn't occupied with other thoughts or ideas.

The main idea behind changing the way you think about yourself is the process of repetition and consistency so you can make strides to reset your default thinking. No, you will never be able to eliminate 100% of all negative thoughts, but you can greatly change your default setting. Before my transformation, 90% of my predominant thoughts and mood kept me down, anxious, and depressed. Today, that number is more or less around 20% of the time, and 80% of the time I am grateful, energetic, positive, and living in the truth of my reality. Creating good habits through repetition is a recipe for success in creating unconscious behaviors that can make things a bit easier. For example, today through trying again and again and again, I have set meditation and exercise as daily habits. I used to struggle with daily, but now I know the benefit and have seen it time and time again.

## The Subtle Art of Not Thinking

Let me know if this is a familiar scenario for you. You're sitting down in your classroom or at your workplace break room eating lunch and a few friendly faces come over to you and say hi and sit next to you. You're reading your notebook or eating your lunch and a conversation occurs around you about what happened last night on this number #1 rated TV show. You think to yourself, "Hey, I saw that last night and thought it was interesting!" Someone sitting next to you says something you agree with and you want to share your thoughts about it. You are trying to think in your head of what you want to say, and by the time you think you have a perfectly formulated thought, the conversation changes to a restaurant that just opened up in town that has amazing food. You then again attempt to create a perfect thought because you remember that your friend told you they went to that restaurant two nights ago, and it wasn't that good. The same thing happens: by the time you're done thinking, the topic of conversation has changed or isn't on the same topic, so speaking your perfect thought wouldn't make sense anymore.

Welcome to living shy. Here's the real irony in all of this. Throughout my life I didn't even know I was shy. In my mind, I wasn't actually shy on the inside, but on the outside I didn't speak a word because I was too busy talking to myself. You run this cycle on and on and on again and you have trapped yourself inside your own noggin. What's the antidote? Intellectual courage. I'm talking about the subtle art of simply not thinking beforehand and just speaking and trusting that you will say the "right" words. This may seem either super simplistic or flat out stupid. Why? Because you don't trust yourself. You think back to all the moments where you made a fool out of yourself in front of a friend, kids in the classroom, the table at the lunchroom, and you made a mental note to yourself to not speak up.

Why don't you trust yourself? Let me tell you a story once told to me by Ed Mylett, ranked under the World's Wealthiest under 50 People, but was once referred to as shy little Eddie. He said, "Imagine your best friend right now, Rick or whatever his name is, and imagine he calls you up and says hey! Do you wanna go grab tacos at the bar down the street tonight at 7pm? You say yes, I'd absolutely love to do so. You show up at the bar at 7pm at the exact location he mentions, and you wait for 30 minutes. You shoot Rick a text and he says hey man sorry I couldn't make it. Can we reschedule for tomorrow at the same time and place? You understand, things happen in life and make a plan to meet Rick tomorrow.

"The next day you show up at the same bar and time, still no Rick. A bit more flustered you text Rick and ask him what's up? He comes up with an excuse that you know is an excuse, but you still love him enough to agree to meet him the next day at the bar. The following day comes along, and guess what? Still no Rick. You text Rick and he makes a big story as to why he couldn't make it but assures you tomorrow he will be there. You text Rick back and say - you know what? Don't worry about it, I'm not interested in meeting up anymore."

You are Rick and you are also you. That's the nature of trust behind the relationship you have with yourself. Every time you promise yourself you're going to do something or say something to that person, you slowly lose that trust with yourself. That lack of trust eventually accumulates, and you don't even trust yourself anymore. It's so bad that next time you are in the middle of a potential social gathering and you tell yourself to do something that requires a bit of courage, you don't do it.

That's a trust problem you have with yourself. Just like everything in life, nothing is overnight, and neither is the building nor destroying of a relationship. You can view this narrative to empower yourself and realize that just because you have treated yourself in a potentially negative way doesn't mean you have to anymore. You can begin, brick by brick, interaction by interaction, slowly trusting yourself and having the courage to be yourself.

Try it next time you're in a conversation with someone. At first your brain is going to tell you that you are being so illogical and stupid, nobody wants to hear whatever sounds you can string together into a sentence. That's normal. In fact, your mind may even trigger every fear survival response (going back to evolutionary biology) to tell you if you do this you're going to die, and people are going to hate you. Again, that's normal. Using the chapters above of getting yourself into an energetic state with nutrition, proper sleep, and exercise, hopefully you have created a bridge to get over that initial hump and take baby steps forward.

In the chapter following we'll cover the art of meditation, which is unbelievably useful in helping you speak without thinking. It's easy to read a book like this and intellectually understand it, but when it comes to actually understanding and acting in accordance with what I said, without thinking, that's very hard. You can't achieve that by reading; you achieve it by consistency of action and a major shortcut to developing this as a regular meditation practice. Trust me, I know what you are thinking. Mark, I can't meditate because I have bills to pay and I don't have time, or I tried it before, and it didn't work for me because I couldn't get my mind to stop thinking. Relax, put a pause on your thinking for a second, and we will address meditation.

# 6.

# Expose Yourself

"Hey! Excuse me sir. Sorry to bother you but....." ahhhh I messed that up, so sorry to bother you, mumbling this as I walk away from a stranger I tried to start a conversation with.

If you have ever read a book on social anxiety, most professionals like psychologists might start off with this chapter. However, if you have crippling nervous system inducing anxiety like I had, you can't exactly talk to people even if you tried to. You have to start with physiology and energy first. It's the easiest to knock out. It doesn't require you to talk to people. It requires you to move, sleep, and put the right things in your mouth. Easier said than done, but try taking somebody who has mind defeating anxiety, brain fog, and lethargy because of that and telling them to go up to random people and talk to them with the advice of "just try harder" doesn't work when it comes to mental health.

Once you have built a foundation through your body and you're giving your body what it needs to produce the right kinds of hormones and chemicals to operate, it's much easier to begin to push and claw your way out of this identity and pattern of behavior you have unconsciously created in your life. Having energy means you can actually be yourself and do what you decide to do and not roll off the couch because your brain blood glucose is crashing because you ate the standard American heavily processed breakfast in the morning. Energy levels are important, and following the biochemical steps in the chapters before will help you with this section tremendously.

I never read a book on how to do this. I didn't find these steps in an article I found on the first page of google; it took me until the second page. No, I'm just kidding. I simply, but not easily, had to sit in the dungeon of my own mind back when I didn't know this information. Back when I didn't have anybody to talk to about how to start talking to people and more importantly being myself. This is what I figured out through days, weeks, and months of failure, experimentation, falling down, and getting back up again and again and again.

## Exposure Therapy

I remember sitting in my college dorm room trying to process the thoughts running around my newly gained brain from the healthy food I was eating that gave me clarity for the first time in my life. I remember trying to make sense of all this, and when you have energy, you are constantly looking for ways to express yourself in the world. I eventually got down a path of thinking where I told myself, the same reps you put in at the gym, bicep curl after bicep curl, you need to do the same thing with social anxiety.

I pulled out a piece of paper from my journal and said, "Hey Mark! Today we're gonna talk to people." Very descriptive and detailed I know, but this was the start for me. The rest of the page read something as follows:

**Challenge 1:** Today, go outside and talk to 5 random strangers.

I went outside, started walking around a bit, and to my surprise, I found a stranger. As I tried opening my mouth, my brain scrambled it's defense mechanisms and told me: Mark, what are we going to say? Oh no, you can't say that. But what if this person hates you? That person is probably busy, and I don't want to distract them. Ah, it's fine; we can just talk to the next person. Darn, missed it; looks like we gotta wait until the next person. And the cycle continued.

As you can see, this was a very ineffective method that didn't do much other than cause me to think I'm an even bigger idiot for trying to do something proactive. I went back to my dorm room, closed the door behind me, and began planning out my strategy. I realized that such a broad indirect goal of just "talking" was the big issue. I needed to get more specific so I could give my mind a simple and straightforward task to start off with. On top of that, I realized, wait so what if I can talk to a random stranger? Why do I actually want to be doing this? What's the point of me talking to people?

What will my life look like if I can talk to anybody in the world?

This is where I began to realize the importance of having a black and white reason for doing something in your life. I answered that question above and realized this is one of the keys of tapping into my full potential of how God created me to be in this world and the destiny I must follow won't work if I can't talk to anybody. Social anxiety and speaking with others became my deep rooted WHY and purpose for doing the things I do today.. Once I sat down and wrote out my reason for doing it, it became a bit simpler.

I went back to my journal and wrote something like this: Today, go outside and ask 5 strangers what time it is.

I put on my jacket and hat, went outside, saw somebody and proceeded to signal my hand to them and say, "Hey can I ask you a question? Do you know what the time is by any chance?"

Stranger: Yeah, it's 11:39am

Me: Ok, thank you. Have a great day!

WOOOO we did it! That wasn't so bad. My nervous system went from extreme periling anxiety to a great dopamine boosting feeling. And I did it, again and again and again, with some sweat and at times my brain getting very antsy, but without too big a problem. I succeeded. Looking back at this now, and as you have been reading this book with me, social anxiety or being shy is not so much being afraid to talk to people.

It's being afraid to present yourself to the world for who you really are at a deep psychological character identity level. Growing up I had such poor self-esteem, such a negative story about who I was and my intentions, as well as a lot of shame building up because I wasn't proud of the person I was deep down.

When you are able to ask a question that is very specific with utility and not aimless and not about yourself or even anything deep, you will slowly begin to see this part of your brain open up. Slowly but surely, this is a good first step in giving your mind a chance to see what happens when you do speak and rearrange those mental models in return. Most people when attempting to eliminate social anxiety may start and end with this practice of exposure therapy. This is just an initial step, not a solution you can slap on and think your social anxiety is gone. This is the most shallow layer you can begin to apply.

Most people that ONLY DO THIS, they only get so far, and then in situations notice they are very shy and anxious and may have an alcoholic drink to loosen themselves up at a party because they haven't tackled the root cause. Again, nothing wrong with that, no judgment, but if you are actually trying to dig into the root cause, and truly shift your ways once and for all, you should continue reading.

Additionally, for the best possible results, you should systematically expose yourself to each layer that Ellen highlighted in the section above. Again, they are, physical appearance, signs of anxiety itself, social skills, and your entire personality or character.

I'll give you another example of an exercise you can do. Growing up, my family did not have a ton of money to spend on non-essentials. I remember wearing the same clothes over and over and over again, sometimes without changing them between days. There were times where I was made fun of by some of the kids in my school who had a ton of their parents money to blow on whatever they wanted. I ended up becoming pretty nervous and worried about what I would wear and how people would react. Eventually, I began to expose myself to this same fear I had over time. I went out and bought a bright pink shirt with floral shorts that were too short along with a pink hat. I would walk around in the most public places possible, like malls and semi-crowded areas, to expose my mind to the fact that a lot of the times people are not going to like how you look. But, never once has someone walked up to me and insulted me and said how dare you wear that?

**Exercise:** I recommend going through a series of steps and layers of exposure therapy. Start with what I first mentioned of walking up to 5-10 random strangers and asking questions:

1. Do you know what time it is?
2. Do you know what the time and direction are to this place?
3. Do you know the time + directions + give them a simple compliment.
4. Give someone a compliment and start a conversation with a random stranger.

## Shyness Alternative Mask and False Confidence

As mentioned in the beginning chapter, being shy or introverted can be a mask or a guard for someone to put up as a defense mechanism to protect themselves against life itself. In doing research for this book, not everyone I talked to was outwardly super shy. In fact, many of the people I spoke to told me that although they are actively a shy and quiet person, they were deep down just putting on a fake mask, like being the class clown or the attractive jock with big muscles or the smartest girl that gets all A's at school. Remove them from their environment and whatever vice they are using to keep that mask up, like alcohol at a party, or an academic environment, or a family gathering, and they are back being shy as their true selves.

Why? Because they haven't truly found themselves yet and are switching around masks to see what fits and what reaction will occur in the world with external validation. For me, social anxiety became the MASK that I put on my face and life so I wouldn't get hurt again. Everybody in this life is different, but you certainly could be wearing a social anxiety mask and not know it. I certainly wasn't consciously aware of the fact that I had indeed done this until over a decade after the series of events had happened that created this problem in the first place.

However, there were a few moments in my life that enabled me to have a false sense of confidence. When I was 13 years old, I stumbled onto the world of the online video game industry and YouTube. I remember back in 2011 when I was just a young man, I had a channel where I uploaded videos of myself playing video games that had 35,000 subscribers. When I was 15, in 2013, I created a multiplayer server for a game called Minecraft to have some fun to play with my friends.

Long story short, this became the world's #1 Minecraft server for a temporary period, and I become relatively rich. To be honest, it wasn't so much the money that gave me an inflated sense of self, but it was the respect and admiration I got being the founder of one of the largest communities on the internet, at one point with over 10 million users. I even remember going to a conference that was unrelated to Minecraft and being recognized by people who played on my server.

At this time in my life, I had so much deep insecurity and low self-esteem for who I was that I created a superficial sense of virtual superiority. Having one side of your ego artificially inflated enables you to mask the legitimate problems in your life. Because you are receiving signs from the world that tell you, you are successful and therefore you don't have anything to fix or repair. In reality, you are just covering it up with how much money you have, your good looks, and the fact that nobody you spend time with is actually real enough to tell you the truth. Other than the fact that going through this made me realize what real success is at a young age, I would rather have had zero success and all failure and adversity for years. A perceived illegitimate version of success gives you all the fluff and bravado to hide yourself from the world, and more importantly yourself, because you can buy whatever you want or wear whatever mask you want.

Ultimately, the character I was playing crashed when I hit rock bottom and decided to change my life around between 2015-16. It wasn't pretty, but neither was the fake mask I was wearing. When you lie to yourself about yourself, you are essentially disassociating yourself from your own life. What are the consequences? Suppressing your emotions, which come back to bite you. Not being able to feel good emotions and feelings. Relying on external vices to give you a cheap sense of low-grade stimulation. And then after that, you have to fake it to the outside world to show people how confident or happy you want others to think you are, which is another cheap sense of short lived pleasure. Faking confidence is a vicious cycle that degrades your morals and ethics every time you have to pretend to be someone in front of people you are not.

It's a trap. Don't buy it because life is short. At the end of your life, on your deathbed, are you really gonna say to yourself, "Wow, I'm so glad I didn't show people that I loved the real me?" Absolutely not. Get clear on the masks you are wearing. Sometimes, it's easier to cling on to a superficial mask than to address the painful truth of yourself or trying to find yourself because you are not certain, which is a good thing. You create yourself through decades of trial and error and you can't just find it.

## Shame: The Ticking Time Bomb

I didn't tell anybody about what I was doing with my life. I was trying to hide the good and the bad from everyone. Hiding from my friends, family, online, the world because I felt as if I didn't know what I was doing and who was I to share? Hiding that I literally couldn't talk to people and had horrible anxiety was holding my neck down 24/7. What I learned is when you hide something from other people, most times you hide it from yourself too. Something happens in life that you don't know how to handle, so you take it and throw it to the back of your mind and lock it in a black box of shame. While this may be an effective short term solution, often times what you will find is that 10 years later, that same issue you thought you hid is now controlling your behavior in what seems like a totally separate environment.

Trying to hide everything in your life creates the ultimate breeding ground for shame to build up. Living a hidden, shameful life leads someone to having no confidence, a bad self-esteem, and, in turn, developing poor mental health. Obviously, I'm not saying you should scream from your balcony everything about your life, but if I could scream one thing from the rooftops it would be to "share your insecurities and fears appropriately." Why? Because I learned that the more you share about that big bad scary monster under your bed, the more that monster loses power over you and actually controls your behaviors and thoughts less. A lot of us don't want to look at the problem head on, so fear obscures the problem in our mind secretly. If you take a flashlight of truth and shine it on that big bad scary monster under your bed engulfed by darkness, you may actually just realize it's no monster at all and just a dust bunny of fear, which is a glitchy byproduct of us living in the modern world alongside our primitive neurobiology.

Looking back, most of my anxiety and social anxiety that developed was because of having no energy or trying to constantly hide from the world about my anxiety and how I'm so weird or messed up because everyone else seems better. This drains so much energy from you. Always needing to remember lies and hiding things about yourself from certain people is so mentally exhausting.

As Mark Twain has said, "If you tell the truth, you don't have to remember anything." Additionally, I believe that most of the problems we have are not actually about the problem. I believe that our problems' problem is shame, not the problem itself. Example - you have social anxiety. Most of us try to hide it from the world, which inherently builds shame. That feeling of being shameful is the emotion that stops you from getting up one day and saying screw this, I'm going to expose my social anxiety and take steps to manage it properly.

We all have skeletons in our closet, but whether it remains an inanimate skeleton or becomes a lively animated monster that can rip you apart is based on how much light you shed on that darkness. On top of that, when you are shameful about your own life and behaviors, you display that message on the outer skin of your body like in *Pinnochio*. You will act as if everyone knows that big bad thing you did 4 years ago. In turn, you will never be sure about who you are in front of others and live a life without confidence about your very character and integrity.

The really bad thing about shame is that if it goes unaddressed, it seeps into your identity, which determines your level of self-esteem, confidence, and your day to day behavior at perhaps a subconscious level.

For example, growing up as a teenager, one of the things I look back on that really built up my shame was stealing from stores. For legal purposes, I will not mention the name of the store, but I would repeatedly shoplift again and again. I honestly lost count on how many times I've stolen. I would grab the item, walk around for a couple of aisles, and when no one was looking, I would put it in my pocket. I would go to the bathroom, unwrap the item from its packaging, and put it back in my pocket and leave the store. This shame builds up again and again until addressed in the background of your unprocessed mind.

As I grew up and realized this was wrong, I went to my parents and told them that I did this and in an effort to right my wrongs, I went to the store I stole from and donated the amount of money I thought I had stolen, times ten, and donated it to their charity foundation. You have to come to terms with who it is you actually are and forgive yourself, say you're sorry to the people you impacted, and slowly but surely you will heal.

**Exercise**: Write down all of the events and things that you think you did back in your past that you feel shameful about and wouldn't tell anyone. Gain clarity over your list, it may take a few days or weeks to truly remember what happened, vividly forgive your younger self who was in survival mode, and personally contact and apologize to the people who were impacted.

## Meditation Will Crack You Open

Have you heard of meditation? Probably. Most of you reading may have never ever thought in your lives you would be at a point where you would meditate well. You might have tried to meditate before but didn't stick with it because you couldn't "clear your mind" or ditched it before you could see the "benefits" or think you don't have to meditate because you're not a hippie. In October of 2016, I began setting a morning routine for myself. I woke up at the same time every day and took part in various activities I deemed highly valuable. One of those was and still is to learn something either from a book or a credible article about a topic I am interested in.

I kept on hearing "meditation" in so many self-help articles, books, and from experts that I finally decided to do a bit more research on it. You know what I discovered? I found that the greatest kinds of people from every corner of the earth, like Oprah Winfrey, Kobe Bryant, and Ray Dalio, all meditate daily. Hmmm.... my mind began to ponder the previous misconceptions I had of a hippie or a monk on top of a mountain humming along all day as an excuse to be lazy and do nothing. In realizing that, I found that my mind created another excuse to get me to unconsciously avoid an unbelievably powerful tool to heal. It was another example of always trying to find the easy way out, or the path of least resistance.

So, one day my friends and I were going to Six Flags for a Halloween trip. During the 90 minute bus ride, I got bored and said to myself, "Whatever. I'm gonna download this app called Headspace and meditate for 10 minutes on my phone." After downloading the app, putting on my headphones and following along the meditation for the allotted time, it seemed like 3 seconds passed by. The alarm for the timer rang and I slowly opened my eyes. Nothing crazy happened, but something felt a bit different. I couldn't exactly put my finger on it, nor do I know how to perfectly explain it with language today, but it was almost as if my backend perspective slightly shifted.

I had gone with a small group of my friends that was supposed to link up with another group of my friends - people that I didn't know. My social anxiety wasn't really active as I was just going with a couple of my best friends I had known for a long time. But, here's the really interesting thing...when we got to the park and linked up with those other people I had never met before, something really interesting happened.

My social anxiety didn't "flare- up" as much as before. Sure, it existed and was certainly there, but I felt a bit more flexibility and fluid than ever before. I even remember asking them questions and laughing at jokes together. Like most things in life, I didn't realize this at the time, but luckily this was good for me and I decided to stick with meditating on this app. I intentionally told myself I was going to stick with this habit as an experiment to finally prove to myself that meditation wasn't for me. Day in and day out, I would wake up in the morning and meditate with my headphones in a corner of my apartment.

Here's the craziest part. Two weeks into meditating daily, I literally thought my entire life was falling apart. It's not that I necessarily had a ton of anxiety on the inside of my mind, but the very structures of what I thought life were on the outside were slowly changing. I'm talking about the internal structures that actually create what we see through our eyes. I could almost swear to God that I was starting to experience more relaxed drivers, or maybe it was because my mind was at ease and wasn't seeing every movement from the outside world as a threat? I'm talking about what makes our immediate reactions when people say things, or we get offended and throw a mental temper tantrum, or are able to negotiate with the conversation going on with ourselves. All of a sudden, I could start to focus on things with mental clarity, which led me to question the belief I had of I'm stupid, and saw myself rise intellectually, speaking in ways I've never experienced before.

Perhaps the most profound change was when I actually began to realize that I had a series of voices and dialogues going on inside my brain at all times. I never realized that, and a friend of mine, Jeff Warren, states: Meditation makes you realize that we all have a voice in our head that's actually running the show.

But even more profound is I became aware that some of the strands and highways of thought that weren't even mine. My brain had picked them up, unknowingly, as perceived key pieces of information for my survival. These linked back to the days in school when I endured bullying and racism, and internalized them as my own voice of who I believed I was, when in fact, this was just a story that my brain was repeating because that's all it ever knew.

It's almost as if I was an onion, with layers on layers of protective coating; but, really deep down, I was a squishy bulb that didn't really represent those other layers I had outwardly worn like a coat or a mask. As I began to meditate every single day, eat healthy, exercise, and sleeping 6 to 8 hours a day, these layers began to shed and fall off. This was terrifying at first, as I felt like I had to hide from everybody in my life while I went through this extremely spiritual quasi mystical experience. It was especially frightening because I had grown relatively comfortable and accepted these layers as my own. Change is difficult, even when it's a really great evolution that's happening in the process. But, just like a caterpillar is unconsciousness about what's happening to it, it prepares it's arrival into the world as a new being, better and more powerful than ever before. We are like butterflies.

Now, everyone's experience with meditation is different. Some of my friends, who are seasoned meditators, almost all talk about the same thing. It's like when you finally shine the flashlight at the monster under your bed and realize it's just a shadow of a dust bunny. Meditation doesn't necessarily calm you down; it changes the very structures of how your brain works and emits thoughts on a moment to moment basis. Eventually, after years of meditating, you can get into a state of mind that understands problems, discomforts, pains, and insecurities; fears will come and go, arise and disappear from your mind on a daily basis. You will come to peace with the flow of paradoxical human nature and appreciate life for being what it is: a wide ranging beautiful and meaningful experience.

My friend, Rob Dube, is an extremely successful entrepreneur. His company is on the Forbes list of America's Small Giant companies, but even at that superior level of business, he began to face some problems with his mind and health. One day, he sat down on a chair and literally did nothing. He began experimenting with his own meditation practice, and a similar experience happened to him as well, where he was greatly able to affect change with the fidelity of his life. Today, Rob runs his own mindfulness retreat, author of a book, and teacher and instructors to thousands of people on how to do nothing. There are countless stories of people like Rob who fit in the extremely productive, high performing model who weren't interested in meditation, that it wasn't worth the time, but now view it as a major life priority.

I want to make one thing extremely clear. If you can't clear your mind, THAT'S A GOOD THING. So many of those I tell to meditate eventually try it but quit because they can't clear their mind or focus. That's the entire point. Meditation is not supposed to be a peaceful activity like you're floating on top of the clouds. Meditation is essentially the gym for your brain, and when you go to the gym and work out and sweat, and come back after and shower, you feel good. That's also what happens after you meditate; it's going to suck in the moment, but it's a wash for your brain, a bicep curl, a reset button, and for the rest of the day, you might feel better and have more conscious awareness. Heck, there honestly isn't a single morning that goes by where I don't get at least one thought that tells me not to meditate or to quit early. It's all part of the daily process.

## "The point of meditation is not to get better at meditation but to get better at life itself." — ZIVA meditation founder and previous Broadway actress, Emily Fletcher

Today, I use ZIVA's meditation program. It's a short course that teaches you the basic fundamentals of how to incorporate meditation in your daily life without hassle. It's a combination of mindfulness, relaxation, and using mantras to slowly trick your body into deactivating stress and sinking deep into your mind's deep dark caves and corners. I used the Headspace app for mindfulness meditation when I first started. Eventually, I stopped using any apps and just set a timer on my phone. I found this worked for me for a short while and realized that I lacked the education and training to keep doing meditation seriously. There were a few weeks during the summer where I did not really meditate. Man, oh man, did I see the crazy impact that meditation had been doing to my brain below the surface this whole time. Those weeks I didn't meditate, I genuinely thought they were some of the most stressful, worst weeks of my life, even though nothing particularly crazy happened.

I would be nowhere without meditation. The more and more I dig into the science of meditation, where clinical trials prove it reduces anxiety and depression, the more I understand a world today that's busier than ever. It is essential to sit down, shut your eyes, tune out the external environment, and spend time with yourself focusing on who you really are. While it might seem crazy to say this, especially if you are reading this and have never meditated, almost within a few seconds of meeting someone I can instantly observe their energy forces – one of the benefits tightly correlated to a meditation practice.

In fact, a study from 2017 found that mindfulness meditation is equally efficacious in treating social anxiety disorder as CBT (Cognitive Behavior Therapy). Researchers at Stanford found that it's not just about relaxing. In a 2009 study, researcher Philippe Goldin shows that meditation helps people with social anxiety and their public image . Goldin states: "The idea is that if a person has the psychological flexibility to shift freely from one mode of thinking to another mode, then that is a sign of health. It's when we get stuck in certain thinking patterns that our beliefs become maladaptive. Often people will subsequently show up in their 20s or 30s with depression or substance abuse and then if you dig below that you find that what preceded all of that was an internal anxiety about performing in social situations."

To me, meditation is non-negotiable. Of course, there is no universal one size fits all regimen, but as the mainstream adoption of meditation rises, so do the misconceptions. I often hear that "you can meditate while running" or "washing the dishes". Although these activities may be calming and reduce anxiety for someone, there is no substitute in terms of actual brain activity other than meditation.

If you find yourself struggling deeply with meditation, I urge you to rethink your process around it. Tell yourself, today I'm going to meditate for 1 minute. Don't judge yourself because you are constantly thinking all the time or extremely uncomfortable. You are a human. If you are able to shut off your mind, then please write to me so I can have a conversation with you because that's not possible, even for the most seasoned meditators. Another study done by the military in elite service men showed mindfulness meditation is an effective tool for processing information in high stress environments. If I've learned anything, it's that if the military is safely experimenting with anything, especially meditation to decrease stress, improve cognitive function and focus, without reported side-effects, you listen, learn, and apply the practice into your daily life.

Try meditation out. Download an app. Watch a YouTube video. Reach out to a Meditation expert/ guide. Do whatever it takes because meditation truly has the ability to fundamentally rewire your brain, show you to yourself, gain more self-awareness, focus in all environments, and in the words of Sam Harriss, "meditation is preparing you for the worst day of your life."

**Exercise**

1. Open up your schedule and find a 10 minute gap to schedule meditation on a regular basis. I recommend daily, but do with what you can. Again, it's not easy.
2. Write down 5 reasons why you should meditate on a daily basis.
3. If you are struggling with finding the motivation to meditate, maybe find a friend or partner you can collaborate with to meditate together. Or, if you have the social courage, find a meditation class in your area.

# 7.

# Being a Shy Entrepreneur / At Work

At this point in my journey, I no longer consider myself shy. Sure, sometimes if I walk into a party not knowing anyone or in an unknown location, I will feel some part of my brain telling me I don't belong here, and I should leave. However, when I exercise the methods mentioned in this book and am in line with my purpose and intentions of what I am here to do. I am able to tap into my energy stream that is defaulted into anxiety, turned and transmuted it into extreme excitement and genuine love and belonging. Anxiety still very much exists, but it's a matter of becoming friends with it and changing your very relationship with what it means to be socially anxious.

## Managing Social Anxiety at Work

By no means did I immediately start off eliminating social anxiety right away. Even after eating the right foods, not lying to myself and others, exercising, and doing exposure therapy, I still had trouble going out in my everyday life and communicating with others intentionally. I had this experience once of going to an event about technology for business purposes in Boston during the winter. I didn't know anybody at this event and set myself a challenge to go out there and try my best to function like a normal, social human being.

I walk into the event; I see people to my left and right, greeting me with smiles, asking to check my name on a list. I enter through the main hall and see crowds of people happily conversing with others, drinking, eating, and having a great time. My mind sees this and instantly panics; I feel my forehead get hotter than an Egyptian in the summer, my thoughts begin racing left and right, paralyzing me into confusion, discomfort, and the feeling that I need to go to the bathroom. I speed walk my way to find the bathroom, because you know nobody will call you out and ask you why you're in the bathroom. A common theme I have noticed time and time again is going to the bathroom has always been my comfort place, my safe zone that I can go to anytime and relax from the constant gnawing anxiety of trying to talk to people.

I walk across to the food tables, do a double take, and walk to them twice because I can't find the bathroom. All of a sudden, as I'm walking, a random guy comes up to me and introduces himself. This was an older gentleman, perhaps in his 50's, in a full suit and tie and of Indian descent with a thick accent. He says, "Hi, Mark," reading it off my nametag. I awkwardly think, "Wait, how does he know my name? Does he know who I am? Does he know that I have no idea what I'm doing here?" I reply, "Wait how do you know who I am?" He says, "I just read it off your nametag." We both erupt in laughter and break the awkwardness between us. He grabs me by the arm and ushers me towards the food buffet at the event filled with fruits, sandwiches, and drinks.

We go down the aisle and he begins to tell me all about each individual food, even though they were clearly labeled and by no means unique or culturally ambiguous. All of sudden I realize what's going on here. This guy that walked up to me is also super shy and nervous at social events; he's using me, another shy guy, to help not just himself deal with social anxiety, but also attempt to help my own social anxiety. If you're socially anxious, you know exactly who else in the room with you is anxious; it takes one to know one.

I slowly began to realize what this man was doing. I leaned over to him and said, "Hey man, to be honest with you, this is the first event I've been to by myself before and I have no idea what I'm doing here." He stared at me seriously for a moment, and then broke a slight smile and said, "Me too, buddy, but this isn't my first event!" He turns around and continues filling up his plate with fruits and little snacks. He finishes, shoves a piece of pineapple in his mouth, and then goes, "You wanna hear something?" I nod. He begins pointing at one end of the room, and makes a perfect circle and says, "Nobody in this room knows what's going on. But if you can come into this room, any room in the world, with a purpose, intention, and focus, you can help the other people who don't know where to go and what to do."

**BOOM.**

All of a sudden it was almost as if my brain flashed through every time I was anxious at a large social gathering. Almost every single time I didn't have a clear purpose of what I was there to do. I remember then seeing other people who I wouldn't necessarily consider to be anxious, also lead groups of people and initiate and make the event possible; it all started to click. I left my new buddy and began testing this newly found theory out with other people like me at the event. I saw someone in the corner of the room, having a drink, and just looking out to the crowd of people alone. I walked up to him, introduced myself, we had a great conversation, and later we connected with each other online. I realized that I only had anxiety in maybe the first second of that conversation. After that, I realized this was just a chill dude like me and it made for another great human connection. It was also a realization: there's nothing to fear, even if my nervous system is telling me to run.

The hardest part of experiencing anxiety is at the beginning of a new situation. The biggest mistake is using a vice to shift your state of mind, especially in a social setting. What I'm talking about is you know before entering the conference hall, you take out your vape and take a fat rip of any substance, whether it's nicotine or THC. Perhaps the moment you enter the event you go straight to the bar and grab a drink to take the edge off or calm your nerves. For some people it may even be hitting up the dessert table and binging on some brownies, cakes, and cookies to give you a slight sugary buzz. For some of you, it may even be clinging onto and having a single conversation with that one friend you brought. All things/tools/people to cover up the bigger underlying issues that will not get you to move outside your comfort zone.

I don't necessarily have a problem with using a tool to change your state of mind or perspective on life to help you do something a bit differently, safely. I have a problem with someone masking the deeper root problem with superficial shallow solutions that actually make the problem worse over time. I'll give you an example. I am a natural entrepreneur. Ever since I was a kid, I've had trading and selling in my DNA. I've had so many business failures that I've lost count, and a few successes that made me a considerable amount of money and generated influence. Entrepreneurship is one of the most stressful rollercoasters in life, especially if you become successful. Many people think the pressure before you have money and people working for you is at an all-time high when you start.

However, when you have more money than you know what to do with, and people look up to you and rely on you for their family's livelihood, you have a completely different level of stress. The amount of substance abuse in entrepreneur land is insane when it comes to consumption of legal drugs, as well as illegal substances. Daily excessive alcohol, methamphetamines, amphetamines like Adderall, and even opiates run rampant in the *Wolf of Wall Street* and Silicon Valley entrepreneur world, feeding the false hope that money will fix all my issues.

What I learned is that our behavior is largely based on the identity we form through previous experiences and knowledge. For example, it's much easier for someone who is quitting smoking to say to someone who offers them a cigarette "I'm not a smoker" vs "Ah, no thanks. I'm trying to quit." Embracing the identity of the smoker assumes that based on your past experience you will continue falling into the same line of behavior because it's what you think about yourself when you are by yourself.

What's another big reinforcer of identity? Social groups.

Who we hang out with and what we talk about has a massive impact on how we think about ourselves on a regular basis. You more than likely have chosen your friends, based on an unconscious level of comfort, even if you think you didn't, and ended up randomly finding your friends by chance. Truth is, if you want to live life on the edge and face your fears, which is what most people do NOT want to do, sometimes you have to venture out and find new friends. We are always growing through life, and it's okay to find some new friends that do something that you want to be doing.

For example, I wanted to start working out and building muscle, but none of my friends around me were doing that. So, I ventured out and gained a few new friends that do go to the gym and are athletic and active. By hanging out with them, I am reinforcing a new habit or behavior. Understand, this idea can swing both ways.

On top of that, it's also a great idea to slowly begin talking about your journey and mission to conquer social anxiety with your friends. Start with your loved ones first, then friends, and if it organically and appropriately pops up in conversation, your co-workers, boss, etc. By no means do you want to walk up to everyone at work and tell them you have social anxiety and now you're saying Screw Being Shy! What will happen is every time you now see your friend that you have talked to about social anxiety, you will be reminded and socially enforced to keep going on your journey. You certainly should not go around your office stopping by every cubicle and telling people about your journey. In fact, speaking too much on any one subject or abruptly mentioning your problems to people can actually be a sign that you are overly anxious and panicking.

In summary, here's how to deal with being shy at work or at an event:

1. Do not rely on vices to shift your state of mind (drugs, alcohol, substances, comfort, food)
2. Find other "introverts" like yourself and speak with them 1 on 1. If you have networked with enough introverts, introduce them to each other and maybe start your own mini-group of conversation.
3. Be more interested in others, don't focus on yourself. Anxiety always creeps in when you think about yourself. What am I going to say? What am I going to do if this person asks me about this? Flip this on its head by asking other interesting questions and even doing research on who's attending the event.
4. Set a specific intention. It's easy to get anxious when you have no purpose or intention being where you are. Journal some intentions before the event, like can I make 1 person feel welcome. Can I introduce person "x" to person "y"? How can I change the way that one person at this event looks at the world?
5. Slowly but surely begin speaking about your conquest to become more of yourself and less shy. Start with those that you trust the most like a family member or best friend and work your way out appropriately.

This also applies to social media as well. If you don't have anybody to support you in real life, you can turn to potentially supportive people online. It's important to see and get help in-person, but learning where you want to go in life can be done via the internet and even help you get closer to people in person. You can go on LinkedIn, Meetup, Eventbrite, or other websites and search for topics and industries that are interesting to you.

In fact, if you can find a list of attendees before an event, you can research them and connect with them on social media like LinkedIn. If it's appropriate, it might be a good idea to reach out to them beforehand and see if maybe they would be down to talk to you on the phone. Now when you go to the event, you might be put at more ease because you already have a friend or mutual contact you have made. If you are managing social anxiety, it may be a good idea to challenge yourself by going to some of these events on your own.

## Show Yourself to Social Media If You Want

Social media. Some of us hate it; others love it. I stand on the side of it is just a tool you can use for either good or bad, depending on the user. However, social media is a product from technology companies, made by humans, and therefore has legitimate flaws. Perhaps one issue I particularly despise is the algorithmic echo chambers it seems to create. Maybe you search for something on Facebook or Instagram that isn't positive and is quite detrimental or not very useful to your life. Now, because you searched it, every time you open up your phone, all you see is the same thing you searched again and again and again. If you know how to use social media, you can use that same feature for good, to show you positivity time and time again.

Algorithms do not care about human happiness. They are designed to add more screen time to users to sell more products. As you swipe and scroll through the negativity, you are probably comparing yourself to it and putting yourself in a lower and lower mental state. Sometimes you just gotta take a break from social media, unfollow those who do not bring you value, and purposely decide how exactly you are going to use social media to add value to your life. Giving someone who has no intention or purpose in life a powerful tool like social media is not a good idea. However, equipping someone in the right mental state to use social media as a tool for business and networking is extremely powerful if used correctly.

Also, social media can be an invaluable tool to establishing who you are to others, especially for those of us who can be socially anxious at times. How? Social media is like a global loudspeaker system. I remember growing up thinking that I couldn't act like the person I really wanted to be because I'm with people that have already known me as this other kind of person. It's almost as if you feel like you can't change because if you do, those around you will ridicule or mock you for being different in a false way. This is where social media could potentially be a beneficial tool for you to spread a message like a loudspeaker to the entire world. If people already know who you are and what you post about from online, it cuts the small talk and you can jump into conversation worthy topics.

In 2017, I was randomly scrolling through LinkedIn. I came across this video that someone had made about an initiative to spread honesty in the workplace, encouraging people to record a video of themselves talking about a vulnerability. Obviously, for me, when I came across this and pondered the idea of recording myself and putting it on the internet publicly, I concluded that it was a crazy thing to do. However, this did not stop me and after multiple takes, I filmed a 2 minute video on my laptop's webcam and uploaded it. I recorded my video about social anxiety and what I was doing differently to tackle the fear.

I walked away and came back to the video the next day and it had some recognition - with over a thousand views and comments of people telling me how courageous I am. Comments and social validation aside, uploading this video actually changed my whole life. Aside from telling friends and family what I was doing, I kept my little endeavor of reversing my social anxiety and becoming mentally stronger to myself. Not anymore; now, the entire world knows what I'm up to and it's resonating with a lot of people.

If I can use my Instagram account to create helpful, conscious content that someone can watch and implement into their own lives, that's better in my book than posting a random selfie. Even better is the next time I go to an event or social gathering, if anyone knows me from social media, they already have an idea of who I am and what I like to talk about, potentially allowing others to engage in deeper conversation.

Use social media as a way to scale an accurate extension of yourself. Today, some of the most important people in my life I have met off social media because I showed my real self. Now, if you visit LinkedIn, I am well known as the guy who talks about deep, important, real talk. Some of my posts have gathered millions of views and even brought me public recognition when I'm randomly walking the streets. Overall, I'm truly grateful for the way social media, especially LinkedIn, has given me the opportunity to accurately represent myself for who I am.

However, there is a much darker side to branding yourself and using social media to establish an identity. Many people that start to do this take a sharp right turn and end up perpetuating a negative identity. You start posting pictures of you partying and drinking and you begin to attract like-minded people. The next thing you know, you've forgotten the reason why you started doing this in the first place. And the perpetuation of this identity you have created on your phone becomes the priority over your true self.

The next thing you know, brands and companies are reaching out to you, asking to sponsor your Instagram for $500 a post, and if the post gets more reach, you get paid more. You start to do some research and notice a pattern of if you want more views, show more of your skin. Now you are creating an identity that doesn't reflect who you really are and it's living a life of its own. Next time you are in public at an event or party and get recognized, it might not yield the best results, especially for someone who has social anxiety.

I would also advise you to not randomly yell from the rooftops to the entire world about all of your deepest and darkest secrets. If you are comfortable or at least just a bit uncomfortable, it's fine to share what you are able to on social media or at work with others. At the end of the day, unless you are writing a book like this, you don't want to give people every single detail of your life. The point of sharing online should be to establish an identity that people can know offline but also to add value to others. Why would someone read or watch something that they can't benefit from?

## Harnessing Shyness as a Superpower

A couple of years ago, I told a friend of mine that social anxiety and anxiety in general is now my superpower. He told me, how dare I say that when there are people suffering from anxiety and can't live their own lives. I responded back by telling him that's exactly the point. By trying to somehow eliminate or defeat anxiety forever is a lost cause. Your brain is the only entity on earth that knows everything about you: your weak points, your deepest darkest secrets, everything; it actually knows more about you than you know about yourself. You cannot just brute force think your way out of social anxiety because that will not work. You must learn how to harness anxiety as a superpower or else it will be your worst weakness. Below lies a summary of the major outline of this book to get you moving on the track away from shyness and more towards yourself. Feel free to go back to the previous chapters to get a more detailed links on the information and exercises.

**1. Your Death** (Inspiration)
Start with the end in mind. From the moment we are born here on planet earth, we are all diagnosed with a deadly disease: Death. We can try to unconsciously run away from it or consciously come to the fact that we will die one day. Everything and everyone we know will no longer exist according to our awareness.

Do you really want that last altercation with your kid or partner to be your last? Do you really think you will be sitting on your deathbed and saying, Phew, thank God I didn't talk to anybody and get embarrassed. Absolutely not. The #1 regret in those dying is living somebody else's life. Don't die with the unlived version inside of you, whether you are young and have plenty of time, or even if you are 75 years old.

Write out your tombstone. What impact you want to have on the world when your body and blood is gone and it's just what you created for others to experience.

## 2. Check the Box on Biochemistry

It doesn't matter how many books or articles I've read about how to change my mindset. If I have slept for 4 hours, not exercised or stretched my body, haven't meditated or written down my thoughts to gain clarity, I've been drinking alcohol and haven't eaten a vegetable in a while, I'll probably be anxious even though my life at a macro level is good. Everything I've spoken on from shame to the truth are at times simple yet difficult elements to embody in life due to the amount of change required. Now, changing up your eating habits or how you sleep might also be a bit difficult for you, but it is almost black and white. It's an easy thing to check off the list to get out of the way rather than exposing yourself to the world.

- **Food.** Eat whole natural ingredients that come from the ground or have been walking on the ground or swimming underwater. Avoid processed chemicals, oils, sugars.
- **Sleep.** Treat your sleep as seriously as you do spending time with your family or working. I schedule sleep on my calendar. Don't drink too much caffeine and keep your mind focused on just sleeping, not overthinking, because that doesn't help.
- **Exercise.** Incorporate regular strength training alongside a healthy mix of cardio. Don't just move in the morning; schedule walks at lunch time, and mini 5 minute workouts you can do throughout the day.
- **Drugs.** Get very clear and honest on what exactly you are putting into your body. Sugar, caffeine, alcohol, and cannabis are some of the most abused substances of our society that keep us lazy and fat and open the door for dysfunctions with physical and mental health. What pain are you using this substance in the first place to cope with? Sometimes we can't do it by ourselves and need professional rehabilitation.

Knock out these boxes on your biochemistry because anxiety could potentially be a side effect of your body suffering and not getting the right nutrition. Take care of that and we can move on and address the other layers.

## 3. Understanding the Truth and Evaluating your Relationship with Pain

What is your real destiny here on planet earth? Were you put here to not open your mouth and not connect with your fellow brothers and sisters? What brings you the most pain in your life?

If you aren't honest with yourself about yourself on who you really are and what you like, don't like, your intentions, and how you want to spend the rest of your life, there's no point in moving on unless it's from a place of genuine truth. This isn't exactly a simple concept to communicate, but it's well worth sitting down with your shadow self and figuring it out. Truth starts from the inside and outside. Don't lie to others, don't lie to yourself, and don't lie to the universe. The only person you are fooling is yourself.

Every time you tell a lie to someone, or even yourself, you are creating a false version of yourself and projecting it forward in reality while shoving the authentic you to the back of your life. Lying is not worth the consequences of being dissociated from your own life, unable to feel the highest of emotions like love and connection, while also delaying pain into the future.

Evaluating your relationship with pain is hyper critical. Understanding the connections we have made on what we do when we feel pain can be illuminating. Pain can cause us to put up masks and suits of armor to protect ourselves from the outside world. That really alienates us from our true self. I used social anxiety as a mask to hide from the world. I also used tools like overeating food and eating drug-like pleasure inducing foods, immersing my mind in video games and TV 24/7, and simply trying to avoid pain. I wouldn't put myself in situations where I could grow and evolve. This just delayed the inevitable pain of facing my true self.

### 4. Learn the Social Skills and Apply Them

Unfortunately, many of us are not so intuitive when it comes to how we should act and treat others in our modern busy world. Not because there's anything wrong or inhumane about us but because we were dealt a bad hand in life and just need a bit more help at it than others. I bet you don't have a problem sitting and working alone, being a potential introvert, or being a shy person. However, someone else might have that as their main problem and don't know how to be alone with themselves. You should NOT sit down in your room alone and complain how you can't talk to people and your social anxiety is ruining your social life. You should sit down and actually build a plan as how you are actually going to do this. How do you become a NOT shy person? You learn how a non-shy person talks, communicates, and socially operates in the world.

Research and practice everything there is to know about body language, posture, facial expressions, physical touch, vocal tonality, annunciation, and eye contact. It will seem very weird at first and not natural to change your social behavior on a regular basis. You might feel this for 6 months to a year. It really depends on each person, but eventually it will be who you are. You are not faking anything. Depending on what age you are, your mind and body may be unfamiliar with other behaviors. If you do anything for 24 years straight and then all of a sudden switch, it's going to feel weird and unfamiliar no matter what. Keep learning, researching, and applying and you will see positive results in the way others perceive you because of how you communicate verbally, physically, and vocally.

In combination with the previous pillars and combined with meditation, you should begin to slowly and systematically expose yourself and experiment with not being socially anxious. Follow the exposure therapy steps highlighted in previous chapters and always challenge yourself. Make it a goal to speak with ten strangers a day. Make yourself go to an event by yourself on a monthly basis. Document your challenges and issues on a daily basis, and keep track of what you are doing because it is incredibly easy to slip back into your old behavior while experimenting with the ideas in this book.

## 5. Put Yourself in Systems and Understand Life is 24/7

**"You do not rise to the level of your goals. You fall to the level of your systems." – James Clear, Author of *Atomic Habits***

You need to create systems that can reinforce the good habits you want to build. Doing something new for the first time and then forgetting about it and never having the consistency to do it daily doesn't take you that far in life. Find a reason to keep going that is not just tied to your own little life but to things like your family, business, and organization. Instead of being selfishly motivated to just grow and develop for the sake of yourself, attach your why to people that you love and movements you are deeply inspired to create.

When I was first starting my journey of self-development and tackling life head on, one of the first things I did was start a business. Now, you do not have to do this, but I have started many businesses in the past and it's something that I'm good at. More importantly, it's not just about me. Making money is great, but putting yourself in a system like a business where you have staff, clients, strategic partners, etc. that rely on you every day makes you bigger than yourself. Starting a business is a rollercoaster of stress and emotions, and while it has definitely strengthened me, I do not recommend it for everyone, especially, if you feel you are not in a great place, mentally speaking. Starting a big venture like a business is most likely going to make you more tired, burnt out, and drained. It's important to make sure you are standing on a solid foundation before you go out and try to do something difficult.

The next system I created for myself was starting my Humans 2.0 podcast in the summer of 2017. I was feeling especially stressed, confused, and a bit unmotivated on my journey at that time. Sure, I was experiencing life from a new lens, but don't be fooled, most people don't do this for the reason that it's extremely hard, yet rewarding. However, I came up with an idea to begin to systematically surround myself with the world's top experts, leaders, and change-makers I wanted to learn from.

So, I started a podcast and solely used it as a tool for my personal development. At times, I didn't want to learn, but I knew I had a guest interview to prepare for next week and had to read the author's book. There were times when my social anxiety was flaring up and I didn't want to talk to anybody, but I had an interview scheduled in 13 minutes. At times I wasn't motivated to keep the podcast or even my own learning moving forward; but, then I would get 16 emails from people like you who listened to my podcast and changed their own lives around.

Additionally, aside from systems, you must realize the importance of the fact that life never ends. Whether you are a billionaire or a homeless person, we are all given the same amount of time in a day. A lot of people believe that one day they will have enough money, or are free with no one telling them what to do, so they will finally be happy and spend the rest of their life on a beach . This is a false paradigm that the human mind creates as a fantasy or some destination goal to arrive at to motivate you to do the work in the present moment. It's very useful for motivating yourself in the short term, but it's a toxic belief that can set unrealistic expectations about life.

Every single morning you wake up, your #1 goal needs to be your overall life calling and purpose and all the work needed to make that life a reality. It's hard. You will be in negativity and darkness almost every single day. You will continue to face issues and obstacles in your life. If you can embrace this mentality, you realize that every 24 hours we are GIVEN is a gift. Statistically speaking, thousands of people every day die in the middle of their sleep. But, you and I are awake and alive to experience life and its range of vibrant emotions, from sadness to loneliness, to extreme moments of love and interconnectedness. Good cannot exist without bad. Light without dark. Love without fear. These are the rules of the game. The same way that before you played a video game or board game, there are rules to follow, and if you follow the rules, you can now control the game and have fun.

# 8.

# The World Needs You

Back in 2015 and 2016, when I was at rock bottom, I was fantasizing about my suicide for 2-3 weeks. I would walk the most crime infested areas of Boston and hope someone would walk up to me and try to mug and kill me. On some of those nights, I began to slowly stumble on listening to podcasts. I stumbled onto the Tim Ferriss show. Out of sheer randomness, I listened to Tim talk about the time when he was in college and was also contemplating taking his own life. Tim ended up getting out of it and not committing suicide. If you don't know Tim Ferriss, he is one of the most influential leaders, authors, and strategists who is now leading revolutions and changing the world at scale by the millions. When I heard this from Tim, my mind slowly began to change and shift. If a super successful guy, who in college was in the same exact position as I am, and tried to kill himself... but is now changing the world, maybe I'm not so insignificant after all.

As I did more research it turns out basically every single person that you and I know now that has changed history, a real icon and leader of the people, has struggled with some major issues. All of them, Lebron James, Oprah Winfrey, the Rock, you take your pick, they all suffered from a very serious issue they didn't know how to get out at that time. Yet, today they are leading people by the millions towards positivity, empowerment, and thought leadership. Many of them have contemplated or even attempted taking their own lives, and if they had, nobody in the world would know about them. Imagine how many people's lives have been changed because of Oprah. Now imagine how many people's lives wouldn't have been touched if Oprah didn't overcome her obstacles and issues.

That's you. That was me before I wrote this book. This is the story of the human experience.

Imagine flipping your life script on its head. Imagine being able to change the world, change the people you love, and change yourself better than you could even imagine. You can do it. It's not going to be easy, but it will be rewarding and worth it.

Imagine going back to this book, six years from now, and thinking, "Wow. When I read this book, I was in a completely different spot in my life than I am now." This is the same way I look at what Tim Ferriss did for me, without even him knowing he saved my life.

Take a look at every major obstacle on planet earth today. Climate change, gun violence, terrorism, wealth inequality, bacterial infections, chronic illnesses, poverty, relationship issues, intergenerational disparity, etc. Every single one of those problems is going to be solved by an individual in the world with their own problems who had to fight to bring them to a point of solving major world issues.

Imagine if Alexander Fleming, the creator of penicillin, the first true antibiotic, killed himself or never got past his own problems to be able to create something valuable for the world. Without antibiotics and Alexander's life, we are talking about potentially hundreds of millions of people dying from infectious bacterial diseases.

Imagine if Alan Turing never created the Turing machine, also known as the first computer in history that was able to decipher German Nazi code in World War 2 and report to the allies where German troops and ships were hiding, enabling the allies to defeat the Germans and potentially save hundreds of millions of people's lives.

I can keep going with examples, but there is no difference between you and the people mentioned above, other than the fact that they have just gone for it. Even if you are not the A player or some crazy inventor or leader, you could play an integral role on the team of people who are going to bring these creations that exponentially benefit humanity forward. If you have social anxiety and shy away from human interaction, you will not have the communication skills needed to collaborate with other smart people.

If you have faced social anxiety, being overly shy or introverted too much, this is your opportunity to take advantage of the moment before you. Many people, at the end of their life, figure out that they really should have lived their own life and not just followed the path of others towards regret. It's hard to speak up and be your authentic self in front of others at times, but it is truly worth it.

# Afterword

I hope this book has helped you build a plan to get out of extreme social anxiety and to start building your own life. I want to take this moment to truly thank you from the bottom of my heart for reading my first book ever. I also want to let you know that my door is open for you. I will try my best to respond back to you as the effort you take to compose a truthful message to me is not easy.

All I ask from you is to not waste your time here on planet earth and get busy living your own life. Spread information truthfully and share with others what you have found to benefit you. If you know anyone looking to be less shy and more themselves, please share this book with them. I am going to try my best to get this book into the hands of every child, woman, and man around the world who suffers from social anxiety. I can't do this alone. I need your help.

Please share *Screw Being Shy* with anyone who doesn't want to be shy anymore.

Also, I have created 500+ free podcast episodes you can check out on my Humans 2.0 Podcast via Apple, Spotify, iHeart, Stitcher Radio, YouTube, etc.

I will see you on the other side and thanks again. Look forward to hearing from you :)

Contact me via my website: markmetry.com

Text or leave me a voicemail: 508-925-0261

Send me a personalized LinkedIn connection request!

Shoot me an Instagram DM @markmetry.

Tweet me @markymetry

# References

Aiguo Wu, Emily E. Noble, Ethika Tyagi, Zhe Ying, Yumei Zhuang, and Fernando Gomez-Pinilla. "Curcumin boosts DHA in the brain: implications for the prevention of anxiety Disorders." *Biochimica et Biophysica Acta*. Vol. 1852, Iss. 5 (May 2015): 951–961. Published online 2014 Dec 27. doi: 10.1016/j.bbadis.2014.12.005

American Addiction Centers. "The Connection between Anxiety and Alcohol." Ed. Meredith Watkins. americanaddictioncenters.org/alcoholism-treatment/anxiety. 2019.

Amminger, GP, MR Schäfer, K Papageorgiou, CM Klier, SM Cotton, SM Harrigan, A Mackinnon, PD McGorry, and GE Berger. "Long-chain omega-3 fatty acids for indicated prevention of psychotic disorders: a randomized, placebo-controlled trial." *Archives of General Psychiatry*. Vol. 67, Iss. 2 (Feb. 2010):146-54. doi:10.1001/archgenpsychiatry.2009.192.

Antinori, Anna, Olivia L. Carter, and Luke D. Smillie. "Seeing it both ways: Openness to experience and binocular rivalry suppression." *Journal of Research in Personality* Vol. 68 (June 2017):15-22.

Asprey, Dave. "Bulletproof." *About Bulletproof*. Bulletproof.com. 2020.

Cunningham, Natoshia R., Anne Lynch-Jordan, Adam G. Mezoff, Michael K. Farrell, Mitchell B.

Cohen, and Susmita Kashikar-Zuck. "Importance of Addressing Anxiety in Youth with Functional Abdominal Pain: Suggested Guidelines for Physicians." *Journal of Pediatric Gastroenterology Nutrition.* Vol. 56, Iss. 5 (May 2013): 469–474. doi: 10.1097/MPG.0b013e31828b3681

Dias, B., Ressler, K. "Parental olfactory experience influences behavior and neural structure in subsequent generations." *Nature Neuroscience* 17, (2014): 89-96. doi.org/10.1038/nn.3594 Dispenza, Dr. Joe. *Dr. Joe Dispenza.* drjoedispenza.com. 2020.

Eisenberg, NI. "Social pain and the brain: controversies, questions, and where to go from here." *Annual Review of Psychology.* Vol. 66, (2015):601-29. doi: 10.1146/annurev-psych-010213-115146.

Fletcher, Emily. "Meditation to stress less and accomplish more." *ZIVA Meditation.* 2020. https://zivameditation.com/

Friedman, Hershey H. "Cognitive Biases that Interfere with Critical Thinking and Scientific Reasoning: A Course Module." SSRN Electronic Journal. (April 2017). DOI: 10.2139/ssrn.2958800

Hensler, Julie G. "Serotonin." *Basic Neurochemistry* (Eighth Edition), 2012.

Hilimire, MR, JE DeVylder, and CA Forestell. "Fermented foods, neuroticism, and social anxiety: An interaction model." *Psychiatry Research.* Vol. 228, Iss. 2 (Aug. 2015):203-208. doi: 10.1016/j.psychres.2015.04.023.

Jacka, Felice N., Nicolas Cherbuin, Kaarin J. Anstey, Perminder Sachdev, and Peter Butterworth. "Western diet is associated with a smaller hippocampus: a longitudinal Investigation." *BMC Medicine.* 2015 Sep. 8. doi: 10.1186/s12916-015-0461-x

Jonsson, Bo H. "Nicotinic Acid Long-Term Effectiveness in a Patient with Bipolar Type II Disorder: A Case of Vitamin Dependency." *Nutrients.* Vol. 10, Iss. 2 (Feb. 2018):134.

Kiecolt-Glaser, Janice K. "Stress, Food, and Inflammation: Psychoneuroimmunology and Nutrition at the Cutting Edge." *Psychosomatic Medicine.* Vol. 72, Iss. 4 (2010):365-369.

Kipp, Mastin. *Mastin Kipp: Live Your Purpose from Now On.* MastinKipp.com. 2020.

LePera, Dr. Nicole. *The Holistic Psychologist.* https://yourholisticpsychologist.com/about-me/. 2020.

Limb, Charles J. and Allen R. Braun. "Neural Substrates of Spontaneous Musical Performance: An fMRI Study of Jazz Improvisation." *Plos One.* (2008). doi.org/10.1371/journal.pone.0001679

Littrell, J. "The mind-body connection: not just a theory anymore." *Social Work in Health Care.* Vol. 46, Iss. 4 (2008):17-37. DOI: 10.1300/j010v46n04_02

National Institutes of Health. "Alcohol Facts and Statistics." 2020.

https://www.niaaa.nih.gov/publications/brochures-and-fact-sheets/alcohol-facts-and-statistics

O'Neil, Adrienne, Shae E. Quirk, Siobhan Housden, Sharon L. Brennan, Lana J. Williams, Julie, A. Pasco, Michael Berk, and Felice N. Jacka. "Relationship Between Diet and Mental Health in Children and Adolescents: A Systematic Review." *American Journal of Public Health.* 2014 October. doi: 10.2105/AJPH.2014.302110

O'Neill, Casey E., Ryan J. Newsom, Jacob Stafford, Talia Scott, Solana Archuleta, Sophia C.Levis, Robert L. Spencer, Serge Campeau, and Ryan K. Bachtell. "Adolescent caffeine consumption increases adulthood anxiety-related behavior and modifies neuroendocrine signaling." *Psychoneuroendocrinology,* Vol.67 (2016): 40-50.

Pagnoni, Giuseppe. "Chapter 13 - The contemplative exercise through the lenses of predictive processing: A promising approach." *Progress in Brain Research.* Vol. 244, (2019):299-322. doi.org/10.1016/bs.pbr.2018.10.022

Paluska, SA., and TL Schwenk. "Physical Activity and Mental Health." *Sports Med* Vol. 29, 167–180. (2000). https://doi.org/10.2165/00007256-200029030-00003

Pucie, Charles. "Scientists around the world to discover new ways to fight disease in poorest Countries." *Bill and Melinda Gates Foundation.* https://www.gatesfoundation.org/. 2020.

Robinson, Bruce A. "Hell and It's Existence According to Alternative Christian Teachings."*Religious Tolerance.* Patheos.com. 8 Feb. 2018.

Rosenfeld, Daniel L. "The psychology of vegetarianism: Recent advances and future directions." *Appetite.* Vol.131, 1 Dec. 2018: 125-138.

Sartori, SB, N. Whittle, A. Hetzenauer, and N. Singewald. "Magnesium deficiency induces anxiety and HPA axis dysregulation: Modulation by therapeutic drug treatment." *Neuropharmacology.* Vol. 62, Iss. 1 (Jan. 2012): 304–312. doi: 10.1016/j.neuropharm.2011.07.027

Schruers K, T Klaassen, H Pols, T Overbeek, NE Deutz, and E Griez. "Effects of tryptophan depletion on carbon dioxide provoked panic in panic disorder patients." *Psychiatry Research.* Vol. 93, Iss. 3(Apr. 2000):179-87.

Schulte, Erica M., Nicole M. Avena, and Ashley N. Gearhardt. "Which Foods May Be Addictive? The Roles of Processing, Fat Content, and Glycemic Load." *PLoS One.* Vol. 10, Iss. 2: 2015 Feb 18. doi: 10.1371/journal.pone.0117959

Srivatsaa, Sharran. "Sharran Srivatsaa." *LinkedIn.com.* www.linkedin.com/in/sharran/. 2020.

Stoner, Susan A. "Effects of Marijuana on Mental Health: Anxiety Disorders."

*Alcohol and Drug Abuse Institute – University of Washington.* 2017. adai.uw.edu/pubs/pdf/2017mjanxiety.pdf.

St-Onge, Marie-Pierre, Amy Roberts, Ari Shechter, and Arindam Roy Choudhury. "Fiber and Saturated Fat Are Associated with Sleep Arousals and Slow Wave Sleep." Journal of Critical Sleep Medicine. Vol. 12, Iss. 1 (2016). doi.org/10.5664/jcsm.5384

Thurston, Matthew D., Philippe Goldin, Richard Heimberg, and James J. Gross. "Self-Views in Social Anxiety Disorder: The Impact of CBT versus MBSR." *Journal of Anxiety Disorders.* Vol. 47 (2017): 83–90. doi: 10.1016/j.janxdis.2017.01.001

Torres, SJ, CA Nowson, and A Worsley. "Dietary electrolytes are related to mood." *The British Journal of Nutrition.* Vol.100, Iss. 5 (Nov. 2008):1038-45. doi: 10.1017/S0007114508959201

Torvik, Fartein Ask, Tom Henrik Rosenström, Kristin Gustavson, Eivind Ystrom, Kenneth S. Kendler, Jørgen G. Bramness, Nikolai Czajkowski, and Ted Reichborn-Kjennerud. "Explaining the association between anxiety disorders and alcohol use disorder: A twin study." *Depression and Anxiety.* Vol. 36, Iss. 6 (2019): 522-532. doi.org/10.1002/da.22886

University of California - Los Angeles. "Putting Feelings into Words Produces Therapeutic Effects In The Brain." *ScienceDaily.* ScienceDaily, 22 June 2007. <www.sciencedaily.com/releases/2007/06/070622090727.htm>.

Ware, Bronnie. *The Top 5 Regrets of the Dying: A Life Transformed by the Dearly Departing.* London: Hay House, 2011.

WHO Technical Report Series. "Diet, nutrition and the prevention of chronic diseases: Report of the joint WHO/FAO expert consultation." No. 916 (TRS 916). 2020.

Wiss, David A., Nicole Avena, and Pedro Rada. "Sugar Addiction: From Evolution to Revolution." *Front Psychiatry*, Vol. 9 (2018). doi: 10.3389/fpsyt.2018.00545

Young, Simon N. "How to increase serotonin in the human brain without drugs." *Journal of Psychiatry and Neuroscience.* Vol. 32, Iss. 6 (2007): 394–399.

Zanesco, Anthony P., Ekaterina Denkova, Scott L.Rogers, William K.MacNulty, and Amishi P.Jha. "Chapter 14 - Mindfulness training as cognitive training in high-demand cohorts: An initial study in elite military service members." *Progress in Brain Research.* Vol. 244 (2019): 323-354.

Printed in Great Britain
by Amazon